Productive Tactics
for
SHALLOW
WATER BASS

How to Find Them, How to Catch Them

By

Larry Larsen

A LARSEN'S OUTDOOR PUBLISHING BOOK
THE ROWMAN & LITTLEFIELD PUBLISHING GROUP, INC.
Lanham • Chicago • New York • Toronto • Plymouth, UK

Published by
LARSEN'S OUTDOOR PUBLISHING
An imprint of The Rowman & Littlefield Publishing Group, Inc.
4501 Forbes Boulevard, Suite 200, Lanham, Maryland 20706
http://www.rlpgtrade.com

Estover Road, Plymouth PL6 7PY, United Kingdom

Distributed by National Book Network

British Library Cataloguing in Publication Information Available

Library of Congress Cataloging-in-Publication Data Available

Library of Congress 85-82041

ISBN: 978-0-936513-00-3 (paper : alk.paper)

⊖™ The paper used in this publication meets the minimum
requirements of American National Standard for Information
Sciences—Permanence of Paper for Printed Library Materials,
ANSI/NISO Z39.48-1992.

Printed in the United States of America

DEDICATION

To my daughter, Angela Marie Larsen, for bringing me much joy over the years.

ACKNOWLEDGMENTS

I wish to acknowledge the significant contribution of my best friend Lilliam Morse, whose journalistic expertise, photographic and production abilities greatly enhanced this effort.

Thanks go to all the weekend fishermen and professional anglers with whom I've shared a boat. I've learned the "ways of the bass" from them all.

The valuable assistance of the many magazine editors and publishers, newspaper outdoor book reviewers, and numerous friends and relatives that helped to make my first book *Follow The Forage For Better Bass Angling* a success is much appreciated. That positive experience generated the desire to create this book on productive shallow water bass techniques. My appreciation also goes to the interested bass fishermen everywhere that seek more knowledge about their favorite sport.

PREFACE

It is said that the average bass angler spends 90 percent of his time in waters less than ten feet deep. The shallows are, indeed, the home of many largemouth. If the right habitat and water characteristics exist in a body of water, most of the population may be there, regardless of weather conditions.

Feeding in extreme cold or hot weather may be minimal, but shallow water bass do function. "Temperature Shock" seems to draw them tighter to preferred habitat. Various other factors affect the interest of the largemouth in striking a lure, but knowing where they may be found is a beginning to enjoying some shallow water fun.

Locating thin-water habitats does not solve the entire problem. Correct lure presentation and technique will assure the action. This book will consider the places in which shallow water largemouth are found and will focus upon the various types of habitat.

Most importantly, this book will talk productive tactics for use in specific habitats. It will identify particular methods that could be successfully applied to places with shallow waters. *Shallow Water Bass* will help the reader find and catch them!

Contents

ABOUT THE AUTHOR

In 30 years of fishing, Larry Larsen has literally covered the global range of bass in their pursuit. He has caught bass ranging from lakes near the Canadian border southward 3,500 miles to Lake Yojoa in Honduras. His relentless pursuit has extended across the hemisphere as far east as Cuba's Treasure Lake and westward 6,000 miles to the plantation lakes in the Hawaiian Islands.

Larry Larsen's angling adventures and research on the black bass have been extensive throughout the southern and midwestern states. He has served as a guide on several waters in Florida and in Texas and currently lives on Lake John in Lakeland. He frequently fishes shallow waters where he has caught and released well over 100 bass exceeding 5 pounds, primarily on artificial lures. His personal best largemouth weighed over 12 pounds, and the top lunker hauled over his boat's gunnel hit the scales at 15 pounds, 3 ounces.

Writing about bass fishing for over 14 years, Larry Larsen has studied all aspects of the fish, and the ways to catch them. The author has been a frequent contributor on bass subjects to *Outdoor Life, Sports Afield, Fishing Facts, Field & Stream*, and *Florida Sportsman*. Over 350 of Larsen's magazine articles on bass fishing have been published in 30 different publications, including credits in *Bassin', Bassmaster, U.S. Bass*, and other major outdoor magazines. His first book *Follow The Forage For Better Bass Angling*, was acclaimed by outdoor scribes throughout the country and proved to be a big success with bass anglers everywhere. That *Bass Anglers' Guide To Understanding Feeding Activity And Improving The Catch* is still helping readers become better bass anglers.

Larry Larsen's photography has appeared on the covers of many national publications. He is a member of the Outdoor Writers Association of America (OWAA), the Southeastern Outdoor Press Association (SEOPA), and is currently President of the Florida Outdoor Writers Association (FOWA). He is a graduate of Wichita State University and has attained a Master's Degree from Colorado State University.

Larry Larsen and the focus of his pursuit.

Very few other professionals in this country have written more on the bass. His writings detail highly productive fish catching methods and special techniques. He believes in explaining to readers the latest and very best tactics to find and catch bass anywhere. The basis of finding shallow water bass and using the appropriate techniques to catch them is presented in this book as an extension of that philosophy.

Anglers that apply the information contained within these covers, on marshes, estuaries, reservoirs, lakes, creeks, or small ponds, will greatly benefit. The book details productive tactics for both the novice and weekend "expert" to apply to their thin-water angling. Numerous photographs and figures help define the optimal locations and methods to go about catching America's most popular game fish.

INTRODUCTION

SHALLOW WATER CONCEPTS

CATCHING SHALLOW WATER largemouth is not particularly difficult. Catching lots of them usually is. Even more challenging to most anglers is catching lunker-size bass in seasons other than during the spring spawn. It doesn't have to be though.

Most professional anglers, many guides, some weekend fishermen, and even a few outdoor writers have learned to consistently catch bass of significant size. They are smart enough to study the current conditions of a lake or river and quickly develop a concept to establish a productive pattern. They know of the relationship between the vegetated areas and the largemouth bass.

Numerous patterns have been successful at one time or another for most anglers. Exploring all possible shallow water patterns is not the intent of this book. Teaching a fisherman, whether beginner or "weekend pro", to develop a systematic approach to consistently locating largemouth, is my focus. If the reader can understand the concepts presented herein and then utilize them while on the water, he should become a better angler.

These pages explore the various water types found throughout the country. They address shallow water structures and present ways to locate concentrations of fish, and techniques to increase the size of your bass catch. Part I sets the "global" stage for discussions of specific habitat in Part II.

If you only have time to thoroughly read one chapter, then consider Chapter 8, Larsen's "Flora Factor". The basis of a productive shallow water fishing system is detailed in those pages. A complete analysis procedure, including the theory and understanding behind each component, is presented. Those "words of wisdom" should be worth the price of the book.

Shallow water cover is usually full of aquatic insects which attract small forage fish, and although the hang-ups in more densely vegetated areas may frustrate the caster, more bass are available.

14

Most of the concepts, in part at least, are not new; the detailed explanation of an analytical procedure to develop productive patterns is. Try to understand the reasoning behind Larsen's "Flora Factor". You'll be a better angler for it.

Location considerations and specific techniques to take bass from shallow water cover are presented in the second half of this book. Each particular type of habitat is explored. Common and unique methods to use in specific habitats are presented.

Over twenty figures illustrate graphically many of the techniques presented in the book. Photos are used extensively to further help the reader develop an understanding of the concepts presented.

Once bass are located, presentation in aquatic vegetation is often the key to taking huge stringers of fish from the so-called "weed-choked" waters. The really good anglers are seldom puzzled under such circumstances. They can catch fish from highly vegetated waters. The shallow water plant life is here to stay, and if you expect to consistently catch (and release) a bunch of bass, you'll have to learn to fish that habitat.

CHAPTER 1

MARSHES AND SWAMPS

THIN-WATER WETLANDS FOR NEGLECTED BASS

MANY MARSH AREAS and small sloughs exist around the country. Some of the better spots cannot be seen from a bayou or dike, and most have seemingly no approach by deep water. One often has to "blaze" a trail to these, through marsh underbrush and thick vegetation which may stand head tall.

You won't find a lot of people back in the shallow marshes either because it is often a lot of hard work to reach the right areas. The waters can be exceptionally clear. There aren't usually a lot of big bass in these waters but don't be too surprised to catch an occasional one. The majority of marsh bass will run up to 1 1/2 pounds.

As expected, wildlife of all kinds thrive in the shallow marsh plain. Alligators inhabit these areas, in addition to raccoons, armadillos, bobcats, wild hogs, deer and snakes. This is particularly important to those of us who wade such areas or use very small boats. Fortunately, my eight-foot Water Spider has an ample free-board.

Marshlands exist all along the Gulf Coast and lower Atlantic, where bayous abound. Marshes usually are present in the flood plain of most major river systems emptying into salt water. Marsh, swamp, and "prairie" potholes are typical of many natural lowland waters that have difficult access.

Shallow, thin-draft, flat bottom boats are probably the best means of transportation in a marsh. They can be poled, pushed, or pulled through the extremely shallow "wet spots" to reach slightly deeper, more productive waters.

Many wildlife refuges are marsh-like and it requires special effort or transportation to get to productive areas. Marshlands exist all along the coastal plains, and some major river systems that empty into saltwater also have their beginnings in swampy, lowland areas.

PRAIRIE HOLES

Many natural lakes are surrounded by "wet" prairie marsh. During normal water conditions, the shallow prairie may have water over most of it. Some holes dropping in depth to 6 or 8 feet may be present for the adventurous explorer with a lightweight boat.

Grass is often abundant throughout a prairie section and it may be, for the most part, impenetrable. Boat trails may exist in some areas. When drought conditions are present though, those boat trails may be useless. Marsh holes are then inaccessible to all, except perhaps to those with 4-wheel drive swamp buggies. Many of these holes might not be fished at all for a couple of years, so big bass may be waiting.

Southern guides have caught big fish from many open water "holes", and credit goes to the alligator for making such waters great. Since early days, huge gators have burrowed their way through the

18

shallow grass patches to their lakeside residences. This constant traffic has kept down growth of aquatic vegetation in several of these areas, making for slightly deeper water and the formation of small coves.

A marsh's highly unusual, "irregular" shoreline is often the result of alligator movement and bass love the custom-built terrain. Seldom does there appear to be evidence of an alligator problem, only the benefits from their earlier presence. The reptiles still exist in swampy prairies around the Deep South, but they pose little consequence to the bass anglers.

MARSH COMPARTMENTS

Freshwater marshes are often compartmentalized. Bass fishing within them can be excellent during high water levels. The water level may also be manipulated by control structures in some levees. A periodic "drawdown" to control aquatic weed growth is often used. When the gates are open, the shallow portions dry out and so does the bass fishing.

A refuge normally consists of impounded marshes and lagoons. The water may be brackish and is generally shallow. Waters in the interior of most refuges contain a good population of bass though. Many are small, but occasionally nice lunkers up to nine or ten pounds are hauled from the swamps by knowledgeable fishermen.

Often, points of access are by dikes which have narrow car trails (sometimes paths), winding over the refuge. These trails, usually built to aid duck hunters in reaching blinds, provide convenient bank spots for land-bound anglers.

BLACK WATER SWAMPS

Swamp land waters can be very dark from the tannic acid emitted by cypress trees and other flora. In dark waters, anglers can generally catch more fish. The poor water clarity covers up angler mistakes, and we all make them. Fish are usually closer to the surface, which allows fishermen to have a better chance at fooling some of them. Since most fishermen are better "catchers" in shallow water, their opportunity to battle some fish is improved in the low visibility waters.

Shallow swamps are often crammed with lily pads which provide the necessary ingredients for some exciting bass fishing. The pads are often the only cover in the neglected waters. The successful angler can avoid the crowds and catch plenty of bass by learning how to fish marsh waters.

The water depth to cast these lures into should be between 15 inches and 8 feet, according to most successful "swamp rats". Reeds or other aquatic vegetation, along with fallen timber or brush in three to four feet of water, are prime spots. Dark waters are particularly productive in the spring and fall. The edges of lily pads and water hyacinths are good springtime haunts of largemouth bass.

During winter, colder surface water temperatures drive bass deeper. The low visibility water does, however, provide an insulation to the weather. Largemouth bass will remain shallower in darker waters. Don't overlook dark water when the weather cools. Put your lure in it, but be careful. Something may just take it away from you!

FINDING REMOTE WATERS

While fishing any area that has numerous connecting bodies of shallow water, certain things help me find the better spots. An important starting point is the more remote and out-of-the-way waters.

It may not be pleasant to trudge several hundred yards through brush, trees, or marsh grass to fish when there's a nice body of water right next to where you parked your vehicle, but believe me, it's worth it. The more remote and inaccessible the body of water is, the less fishing pressure it gets. And this holds true for all types of water.

To help me find the more remote spots, I will start by talking to other fishermen, or people who live in the area, in hopes of learning something from them. Sometimes a brief conversation can do you more good than a day or two of running around and looking.

Another tip is to get up on a high spot of some type, if possible, and survey the area, looking for water off the beaten path. A friend once climbed a water tower to view a marsh area for new hot spots. From his observation point, he noted several nice swamp ponds which appeared slightly deeper than the other ponds in the area. A few had no noticeable approach, even by water. He had to "blaze" a trail through the underbrush and seven-foot-tall rushes. An even tougher part of his trek later that day was carrying out several bass from the "hidden" marsh.

21

Marsh Methods

To catch a nice string of bass from a remote swamp or marsh, there are several things to keep in mind. If the water is very cold, as it usually is in the spring, and warm southerly breezes have been blowing all week, you may find an area of warm water on one side of the lake. This is the place to fish.

Heavy aquatic plant growth in the form of arrowhead, bullrushes, hydrilla, and pads are indigenous to the shallow marsh waters off the beaten track. Small food particles can often be found in the dense vegetation and largemouth are always nearby.

If the wind has been blowing across a shallow marsh at a good clip, chances are that small food particles and the small bait fish that feed on them will also be on the side where the waves have been piling up. A strong wind will slowly push the surface water across the marsh and warm it in the cooler months. The white caps will oxygenate the water and the bait fish will be there to keep the game fish from starving.

In general, the shallower marsh banks will warm up the quickest since there is less cold water present, and the sun can help by easily penetrating most of the depth.

A Cut Above

A dike bordering a marsh or swamp often defines a canal system on that side. If runouts from the marsh can be found every 100 yards or so, that's an ideal situation.

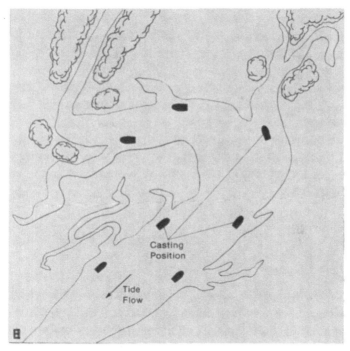

FIGURE 1—*Runouts from marsh areas offer collection of forage and provide excellent bass opportunities. The current from the swamps washes the weaker swimmers into waters more accessible to foraging bass.*

These cuts are especially good under one condition — moving water. This can happen after a rain, when the marsh simply fills up and overflows into the bayous and canals or when the swamplands are extremely low and water is sucked into the canals. The latter happens when tide or floodwaters run full-bore and the canal system's level decreases to a point well below that of the marsh.

Any source of fresh water is a prime marsh spot and usually a great place to find feeding game fish. Food, oxygen, cooler water, and bass are all present in most runoff situations, and remote swamp waters usually have plenty of each.

Currents are influenced by fresh water run-ins and by the marsh's outflow. If there is a heavy run-in and good outflow, the current should also be healthy. As the current moves, it pushes and pulls at the water sitting in the marsh, causing some turbulence. Weaker forage specimens are swept out of the extremely shallow areas.

Rainfall, huge irrigation pumps, locks, or other intermittent causes of flow movement have a great effect on the feeding of lowland bass. The angler that can take advantage of a "drain" situation, whether it's a runoff or a "pull" (suction of water), will often find largemouth angling like little he has experienced. I have fished these at the right stage and have quickly taken limits of schooling bass.

WET FEET

Wading through the shallow swamps is one way to reach remote areas that receive very little fishing pressure. Deep holes exist in such areas, and while some may be difficult to find, many are not. Huge cypress trees in a circular pattern usually denote the presence of deeper waters. Other changes from marsh grass to trees, or varied vegetation, may reveal the location of depth changes. The slightly deeper spots, after all, are the ones that usually hold water year round and provide largemouth the opportunity to grow and flourish.

Much of the successful marsh bass fishing occurs at night. If snakes, gators, and other unseen sounds bother you while you're in the boat, or while wading, night fishing may not be for you. Make sure that your equipment is in good working order before you venture into such areas after dark.

When you're fishing dark swamp water, remember that feeding fish do not rely on sight as much as they would in clear water. You must cast near them to entice that strike. A toss landing two feet away from a swirl (denoting the presence of a bass) may not attract it. Casting the lure right on top of the spot may.

Topwater lures fished slowly in waters of limited visibility are productive. In moving water, the lures can be worked faster against the current. An erratic retrieve is best then.

Fishing in the remote marsh waters can be better than in other, more accessible spots, and the natural beauty is usually unspoiled. All anglers should try to keep it that way while enjoying some fantastic bass fishing.

CHAPTER 2

PONDS AND POTHOLES

MINIATURE BASS FACTORIES TO EXPLORE

SMALL PONDS are everywhere, but the fishing in each can vary greatly in terms of productivity. Selecting one which may produce the best angling may be difficult in a countryside full of them, but knowing what to look for, and where to look, should help.

Most anglers are probably able to see a number of small ponds or potholes from the road during their travels. There are also many more hidden from the casual observer. Just how a pond is used has a direct bearing on how good the fishing might be. Also, how it was intended to be used is important. Those used primarily as livestock water supplies can vary greatly in fish productivity. Generally, the more livestock permitted access to a pond, the poorer fishery it will have.

If the intended use of a pond is as a water supply for fire control, or limited irrigation, it should be less disturbed and the fishing better. A large amount of fluctuation during heavy irrigation will, however, harm the fishery. If the pond's sole purpose is to supply water for farm homes, or create habitat for game, then it should provide some of the best fishing around. The pond and its margins will probably be "unkept", with weeds and other wild growth aiding the filtering of its waters.

The best fishing can usually be found in a pond designed specifically for recreation. Many are planned with this in mind and you should try to search them out. But before you charge up to the farmhouse and ask for permission to fish, many things can be

Shoreline anglers can pick and choose the isolated cover that pond bass often inhabit. Any pond structure can be worked from the bank by a careful, sneeky angler.

checked visually to determine if this is the right water to fish today. You must learn to analyze pond characteristics such as drainage, physical dimensions, clarity, vegetation, and construction.

DRAINAGE CHARACTER

A pond or natural pothole is no better than its drainage area and this is the most important characteristic to analyze in the waters you wish to fish. Investigate the runoff areas above the lake, if possible, and try to get some idea of the entire pond site.

The drainage area may consist of too much cultivated land and erosion has probably resulted in partial silting. Determine the size of the drainage area from the "lay of the land". Usually, the actual water level will give you a good indication. If it appears shallow, using the size of the dam as a reference, then the drainage area may be too small. The pond could certainly dry up in the middle of the summer or in drought conditions.

28

The drainage area is too large if the pond is usually full to the "brim" and appears to be at a flood stage most times of the year. With such a large watershed area, excess water has probably brought in too much silt which disturbs the balance of fish food. A surprisingly large amount of silt is deposited in farm ponds even from better grassland pastures.

Better ponds will have watersheds with grass or other types of permanent vegetation around them, which usually assures water clear enough to sustain a good fishery. If the drainage area is too heavily crop-oriented, the pond could be full of silt and it doesn't need to fill up entirely with silt to be lost. A loss of only 25 percent of water storage capacity could make it useless for fishing.

PHYSICAL DIMENSIONS

Ponds of less than one-half surface acre are usually too small to contain many sizeable fish. Look for ponds which have at least 3/4 acre of surface water. Larger waters are great for fish production but they are not necessarily better than a small 2 to 3 acre pond.

Size may depend largely on the amount of rainfall in the area and this can be extremely variable. Other factors also interact to determine the size of the pond. Composition and type of soil and subsoil, the slope, and the type of vegetation determine the available runoff.

When the fishing pressure is heavy on the waters you are analyzing, try the largest pond. It will be the best equipped to handle the traffic. According to fishery biologists, a pond should generally be able to produce (and lose) 50 pounds of fish per acre each year without hurting the water.

Analyze the depth of the pond by scanning the shore terrain. In general, it should contain some water depths of five feet or more for good bass production. If the shoreline is rugged with steep banks and sharp points jutting out, it will have adequate depth. If the pothole is mainly round in shape with no points or coves, it definitely needs to be checked out for adequate depth.

The depth of a pond can be determined by scanning shore terrain. Ponds with very heavy cover offer great bass fishing, even to the ultralight angler. Highly vegetated ponds are indicative of plenty of nutrients washing down from the drainage areas.

Many times you can tell what kind of fishery a man-made pond might have by noting the construction of the dam, spillway, etc. The "ideal" pond should have a dam that is neither too narrow, nor too steep. A key point to observe is how much erosion has occurred on the face of the dam. If it is extensive, then the dam is a poor one. The erosion will soon cause the dam's loss.

A good spillway is well sodded and lies a couple of feet below the top of the dam. It will be located away from the dam (earth fill) and not at one end of it. It should be designed to take water out in a wide sheet.

POND WEEDS

Some vegetation is needed but too much in a shallow body of water may be undesirable. Often, this weed growth becomes so dense in clear, tiny waters that it may offer too much protection for small fish. Too many cattails, water lilies, or lotus can be as undesirable as a floating mat of scum or moss. Most of us have seen ponds or potholes which were completely choked with aquatic plant life, and know that the fishing is usually poor.

Adequate vegetation actually reveals fertile waters. The growth of microscopic plant life and algae stimulates the growth of small animal forms such as crustaceans, insect larvae, etc., which feed on plant life. In the presence of an abundant food supply, these tiny animal forms grow rapidly and provide food for small fish. The small fish, in turn, serve as forage for the larger predator fish which we are after.

In shallow waters with too much vegetation there are other problems. In the late, hot summer there is often a loss of fish. When the vegetation becomes mature and dies, the decomposition requires much oxygen, leaving the fish with less than they require.

An important characteristic of better ponds is relatively clear water. That water is cooler, because it absorbs less sunlight, contains more oxygen, and provides a more suitable growth of most small organisms.

Extremely muddy water could interfere with successful spawning of bass. If the water that you have your eye on has a turbid condition after rains and it continues for more than a week, then you can usually cross it off your list. The soil in the runoff area could be heavily clay-based and minute particles carried into the pond during rain could remain in suspension, causing an almost permanent turbid condition.

Pond characteristics vary substantially and it may be difficult to find all of the ideal conditions. Certain waters, however, will have enough of the right characteristics to provide plenty of bass action.

ANALYSIS AND AESTHETICS

All characteristics of the pond should be analyzed to arrive at a valid opinion. Certain waters will be strong in some areas and weak in others. The perfect pond may not exist, but many are close enough.

Ideal conditions would include little water level fluctuation and the same amount of water coming into it as that which evaporates. The pond that I'm looking for has: an adequate but not too large drainage area in permanent vegetation, depth of at least 8 feet, sodded spillway and dam, entire pond area fenced, relatively clear water with visibility of 2 feet, adequate cover such as lily pads, stumps, rocks, etc., water surface of 4 or 5 acres and, of course, stocked with Florida bass!

If aesthetics do anything for you, you'll find out that the smaller ponds and potholes are generally prettier. Small natural ponds may have cypress trees surrounding the lakes in 1 to 5 feet of water, while others are simply pockets in pine forests.

Some of these small ponds have boat ramps, but generally there are no fish camps or marinas to be found. It is often necessary to bring your small boat with you, or to wade. I'll usually take my 8-foot Water Spider boat to these ponds. I can sneak up on plenty of bass in most of the unnoticed waters.

SIMILAR STRUCTURE

Structure in shallow water has the same effect on bass as does structure in a deep lake. It's all relative.

Most of my beginning bass fishing (in the late 50's) was in a shallow farm pond of barely six-foot depth. This pond had what we now call "structure". Several dead trees protruded from the muddy water, defining the old creek bed running through the pond.

It was in this five foot deep creek bed, surrounded by tree-studded three foot water, where I caught my first seven-pounder. It was late spring, and I was working a balsa plug along the brushiest tree at the creek bed's edge when the bass engulfed the lure. The partially submerged brush along the old creek channel was super structure for the one-acre pond's bass, and all our good fish came from this area.

Prairie potholes are often isolated in a sea of submerged grass. But they can be hotspots. A narrow, pointed craft, such as a square stern canoe, is ideal for reaching such places. Cast into the nearest weed edges but don't neglect the center of a small pothole. Worms or spinnerbaits, are fairly weedless for this type angling, and very productive. Quiet angling with a "twitching" injured-minnow plug will often provide a chance at the biggest fish in the hole.

LURE SELECTION

Waters such as ponds and potholes normally possess a smaller forage-base size and lure selection should take that into account. You may have to scale down the length and/or girth of a plug, for example, to reap the best results. Prior to the lure selection, you should consider the fishery composition and size of predominant forage. That's the advice from this believer of "big baits for big bass".

Remote waters often contain numerous small, keeper-size largemouth, and occasionally a trophy can be pulled from the lightly fished areas. A soft plastic worm rigged Texas-style is extremely productive in highly vegetated ponds.

A pond with sparse cover can be fished with almost any weedless lure by the accurate and careful caster. In this category, you just cannot beat a soft plastic worm rigged slip sinker style. I prefer to use either blue or darker-colored Salty Sensations made by the Fishin' Worm Company in Lakeland, Florida.

One of the best lures for small pothole fishing is the light, balsa wood-type. Since bass may be unaccustomed to seeing artificial lures in some potholes, they will strike at most types. The floating minnow type plug has great action and is a strong producer. It may be fished on top, just under the surface or a combination of the two.

Ponds and potholes are scoffed at due to their size, yet many can produce bigger bass than the much larger lakes nearby. Look at the state records and you'll generally find "private pond" listed more than any other body of water.

CHAPTER 3

NATURAL LAKES

IDEAL CREATIONS OF SHALLOW HABITAT

THE MAJORITY of natural lakes are very shallow and fairly round. That's not bad! The more shallow the lake, the easier it is for dissolved oxygen to penetrate the entire depth of the lake.

The "roundness" of a natural lake determines how the wind will affect its stratification. On a round lake, wind from any direction can create wave turbulence and "stir" up the lake into a more homogeneous body. Pockets of dead water (low dissolved oxygen content) will seldom be found in these shallow lakes.

No matter how much we prefer to fish on waters which are protected from the wind, the fact is a healthier, natural lake generally has very little protection from the wind. Fishing shallow, natural waters can be a windy experience for any angler, but the wind can be used to his advantage while working good fish-holding structure.

Many anglers make a big mistake by assuming that shallow waters have only flat bottoms. Natural lake bottoms throughout the country abound with sink holes, rock out-croppings, springs, fallen trees and creek beds. Since such structure provides food and comfort to a bass, understanding how to recognize this structure is important. The problem in fishing most natural waters is that there are just too many great looking spots.

Probably the most important thing a natural lake fisherman can do is learn to read the shallow water and establish a pattern. Many keys to bottom structure exist at the surface, for the careful observer. Small pockets up in heavy cover, such as grass, bullrushes, or lily pads, can be a utopia in a shallow lake and should be explored thoroughly. The scattered light in these areas is what all fish prefer. Small lures can be tossed into such places without creating a disturbance. Too much commotion in a small pocket of water can frighten away fish.

Shallow lakes are, by nature, weedy and generally have some sort of weedline. The weedline points should be worked before any other portion of the weeds. After that, the angler should forget working the entire weedline and start looking at the shore. Many times, the shoreline definition can provide a good indication of an area to search.

In the spring, the bass will be back inside a shallow weedline. After spawning, they'll generally move to the weedline nearest a dropoff and set up home for the summer. However, for those who learn the ways to master the techniques for bass fishing natural waters, rewards can be great!

Tough Stuff Strategy

Many fishermen may pass up the tough stuff and miss out on some exciting bass fishing. Spending more time hung up than working the lure? Vegetation in natural lakes can pose particular problems to many shallow water anglers, and it can mean frustrating fishing.

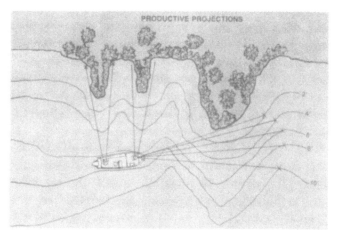

FIGURE 2 — *Natural lakes often have small protrusions. When working such points, cast as far back into them as you can and retrieve the lure parallel and as tight to the edges as possible. Work the longer points at various depths starting with casts to the shallower breakline.*

Snag-infested waters scare off many anglers who are afraid to cast into the middle of the stuff and many feel that they would lose any sizable bass they might get on. Bass are in heavy aquatic growth though and knowing how to successfully fish for them, while preventing most hang-ups, is vital.

Spawning activity is the ultimate purpose of all bass frequenting shallow weeds in the spring but once the bedding is finished, they can still be found shallow for some duration of time, depending on food availability and water clarity. Shallow, sparse weeds in clear, deep lakes may not hold many fish for long, while a tannic-acid stained lake may have post-spawners in extremely shallow waters most of the year.

- **WEED DENSITY**—The length of stay of post-spawning bass in natural waters depends on the density of the aquatic weed cover, in addition to the food and water clarity. The weedier the water, the better its chance of holding a good population of bass. Also, the shallower the lake, the more apt bass will be to take up residence in the thickest bed of aquatic plants available.
- **WEED BED EDGES**—Many weedy, natural lakes in the South have shallow water inhabitants for most of the year. Bass may move from shallow, two-foot beds to heavy vegetation in about three feet of water and go on a post-spawn feeding binge for a couple of weeks. Then they'll likely move to the edges of heavy weed beds (in four or five feet of water) and remain there for several weeks prior to moving to any deeper-water structure that may be present.
- **OVER-ABUNDANT WEEDS**—Weed infested natural waters can be found in all areas and most states have their share. The winter weather can knock the weeds down quickly, but they'll come back again in the spring or early summer. An April day may be just too early to find lily pads at a location where a huge bed of bonnets had existed the fall before. Consequently, some of the better weed fishing takes place in the late spring, just after the spawn.

WEED WAYS

In some natural waters of southern states, weed growth is present throughout the year. A mild winter increases the possibility of year-round weed fishing. In some states, the best time to fish natural lakes is in the spring and early summer. After that, the weed "blanket" may be just too heavy to penetrate with a lure.

Natural lakes that have crystal clear water may be full of aquatic vegetation. Eel grass, hydrilla and other vegetation such as pepper grass, bullrushes, cattails, hyacinths, bonnets and sawgrass could exist in various areas around a lake. Any floating or emergent vegetation could limit the oft distracting water skiing activity though.

Shallow waters are conducive to cattails which often fringe the edges of clear, natural lakes. Frequently such vegetation offers the only cover to the predator bass.

41

Never overlook a natural lake full of moss or algae. Catch these waters in the springtime before the moss has grown and clogged up access. Many natural waters are so overgrown with moss or weeds that there is only a small area in which to fish. A top-water plug, or shallow-running lure which can be retrieved over the moss, should be used.

Poor water clarity shouldn't keep you from trying a lake. Much of my fishing has been in water of six-inch visibility. Generally, try these waters during droughts or after periods of several days in which no rain has fallen. Also, most are clearer before spring rains and should produce best then.

WADE BACK ALLEYS

Many natural waters have three distinct weedlines, one where the shoreline weeds end and another on either side of a bar that skirts the perimeter. Thus, a weedbed lies in front of the shore-based weeds, leaving a small channel between the two. This is usually a deeper trough with sparse weeds bordering it.

Bass use these "alleys" to move along in search of forage. The edges are productive spots to cast and a wade-fisherman can work it most effectively. Pockets lie off to either side of the alley. The successful wader will work these areas slowly and very thoroughly, hitting all irregular features.

Similar areas are produced as natural lake waters rise and cover the shoreline vegetation, leaving those taller weed masses just offshore. These areas are particularly productive on windy days when waves will pound the front face of the weed beds. Largemouth will often lie behind the wind break in the shore weeds, facing into the wind.

Successful waders look for stained-water clarity, hard bottoms and other structural changes that denote bass. They'll cast to the shallow side of any weed mass. They'll work the trough and pockets just off the mass by moving to the most optimal casting spot. Lure presentation is a key to filling a stringer from the back alley.

LURE CHOICES

Spinnerbaits are very popular in the troughs, as well as on the weedline, and an unbalanced lure will become fouled easily in the grass cover. The bait should tip the weeds, which often triggers a strike from nearby bass. Floating, do-nothing and swimming worm rigs are all productive. Small alleys and pockets in shallow cover are ideal for working these slower, more "distinct" lures. Their buoyancy is effective at keeping them out of tangles and in the strike zone longer.

Lightweight lures that are tops for most natural lake anglers are the floating minnow plugs, small crankbaits, small grubs, rubber lures, and little spinners. Shallow water bass will sometimes spook easily and a soft landing, slow moving morsel is the angler's best bet for success.

If the water is exceptionally clear, long rods are helpful. With usually clear water, distance is the prime reason for such equipment. Light lures, thin-web lines, and long casts on natural waters put bass in the livewell.

Many natural lake bottoms are mostly muck though. You can't wade them. For that reason, you can't use heavy weights on a Texas-rigged worm or deep-running crankbaits. In fact, a topwater lure is preferred by many anglers familiar with such waters.

BASS BEHAVIOR

In spring, as plant growth flourishes in natural lakes and pH rises, fishing generally becomes easier because bass behavior becomes more normal (as the pH nears their preferred ranges). When there is an abundance of sunlight and sufficient aquatic vegetation, the pH level should be more alkaline. Often, clear waters have high pH levels. Light penetrates deeper into the water and affects, through photosynthesis, more vegetation.

Correspondingly, pH levels around weedbeds are normally much higher than in the barren areas. Under windy conditions and uniform mixing of pH, the weedbed itself should hold the highest levels of pH. Bass will respond to these conditions by holding tighter to the weedbed.

Cypress trees are abundant in many shallow waters in the South. The tannic-stained waters are a preferred habitat of huge bass.

Natural lakes are normally in areas with high levels of rainfall. Heavy showers in the summer or fall can affect the fishing. Too much rain often increases the pH to a higher than normal level. Bass, in turn, will stop eating. The flushing of any shoreside bayous will slow fishing on the lake's fringes.

Bird behavior can be correlated to bass behavior. At daybreak, scan the horizon for gray and white herons, large birds that feed extensively on menhaden minnows. Then, follow these birds to their feeding spots. There, your plugs will usually garner some bass action.

Watch the movement of coots in the shallows, which can be a tip off to the presence of a big bass. These small, weed-eating ducks will skirt around a large bass on a bed or at the edge of cover and they will look at that bass as they pass around her. Watch the coot's eyes as it swims in an arc, apparently moving around a predator. Keeping an eye on the pH level and bird activity will often clue in a shallow water angler to the general location of bass.

CHAPTER 4

LARGE IMPOUNDMENTS

RESERVOIR REASONING

SHALLOW RESERVOIR WATERS are no different from deeper waters. Contour plots or topographical maps of the areas to be fished are helpful. If none are available, an attempt should be made to make one. Time invested in developing a good contour plot should reap many bass-benefits.

A lot of effort can be spent watching a depth finder hour after hour in waters less than 10 feet deep, but with a newly-constructed contour map, you'll gain an essential "tool". You'll soon forget about your tired eyeballs when a large bass is straining your tackle.

For those who have no depth finder, a particularly easy way to establish presence of structure and make your own topo maps of shallow waters is by wading. This is very refreshing in the summer months. Those shallow lake fishermen without the patience to use a depth finder, can fish as they wade, and cover a lot of ground.

I had some fabulous July fishing one year, due to wading a reservoir, defining shallow bottom contours and structure and establishing a pattern. Under the circumstances, I considered quite a feat the fact that my brother, two friends, and myself found several eager, full-grown bass. Everyone caught many bass between 5 and 6 pounds that week.

Hot and muggy were two words to describe the week's weather. The daytime temperature highs ranged from 99 to 103. The heat, and work commitments of the others, allowed only for 8 a.m. to noon fishing hours.

Wade-fishermen often find bass in the backs of shallow,brush-filled coves. They can thoroughly work the habitat from optimal positions.

We concentrated our efforts on the west one-half of a state-owned impoundment. This portion of the shallow reservoir had an underwater ridge running out into the lake and the total acreage was half covered with stickups. The small dead and rotting trees inundated much of the area.

We trailered a boat to the lake the first morning but soon found ourselves wading to cover the area thoroughly and obtain facts for our contour plots. By necessity, a lot of time spent that morning was unproductive. We were after topo readings first, and bass second.

The lake bottom was mud and with each step we sank into a few inches of silt. The lake had a maximum depth (in the west seventy acres) of about six feet. Thus, wading was not that difficult, and the water helped cool us off. We all spread out and covered as much water as possible, taking notes and making observations on each weed bed point or log where a bass was found.

The muddy water had about one foot of visibility. In other words, we could see our lures as they descended about six inches into the murk before they disappeared. The natural poor clarity allowed the bass to inhabit such a shallow lake and thus make a foot drop a great breakline.

ACTION TIME

The four of us caught 53 bass that day. A Cordell "Big O" plug in a pea-green color and a chartreuse spinnerbait proved to be the top lures for the first two days. We chose the crank-type, vibrating baits due to the poor water clarity and a substantial wind.

The following day found the four of us again chest-deep in the murk, searching for further facts. One-inch long shad were cruising about the lake's surface. Periodically, a small bass would bust them on the surface. We caught several feeding bass by casting to the action, but the shad soon disappeared and we continued our exploration and probing. A total of 67 bass were caught and released by noon.

As we drove home that afternoon, we tried to put it all together. We assembled a map which included all surface structure features (stickups, posts, weeds, pads, etc.). From looking at that sketch, we could determine other potentially good areas. Without the contour plot, much of our time would have been wasted.

All depth data was added to the sketch in the form of contour lines. Three, four, and five foot depths were noted. With our maps fairly complete, we concentrated on the lunker haunts on the third morning. We totalled only twenty two bass including four between five and six pounds. The next morning I took the largest, a 5 1/2 pounder, and Ron landed a 4 3/4 pound largemouth. That day's total was thirty three bass.

FINAL ANALYSIS

The four of us had landed 175 bass in four mornings. A dozen of them ranged from four and one-half pounds to six pounds, and most of the others were one to two pounds. This is not spectacular by any means, but had we not fished that shallow structure, our totals would have been minimal. Several other fishermen on the impoundment had none, which, along with the blistering heat, evidently established the "very poor" fishing report for this particular lake that week!

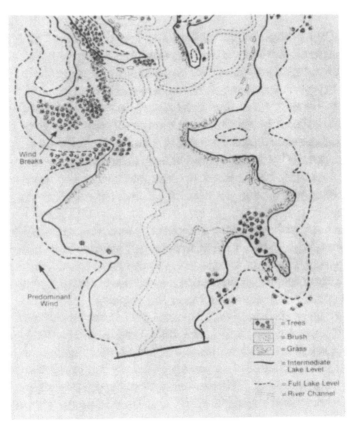

FIGURE 3 — *In shallow impoundments, bass populations will literally explode the first few years. Newly-created waters generally will have excellent color and fertility, plenty of cover-coated shallows, an abundance of forage and many roaming fish that have not yet adapted to hard-to-fish and reach spots. Lush vegetation forms wind breaks to aid anglers on windy days, a feature not found on many shallow, older reservoirs.*

All but two of our lunkers came from a shallow point and along a trough. That's a pretty good breakline! Wading to establish the contours resulted in this find.

Shallow reservoirs similar to this one exist all over the United States. Good topo maps exist on very few, so you have to either take a sensitive depth finder and cover them, or wade. In either case, you often have to make your own.

Take paper and pencil with you and rough out all surface structural features such as pads, grass, trees, piers, stumps, rocks, etc. Learn to read the water. Then make contour plots of all depths and get as much detail as you can. It'll mean a reward in bass if you do your research.

START YOUR SEARCH

Take a systematic approach. Since most of us don't have all the time in the world, we should use it to our best advantage. Lets assume we will wade to establish our contours. Look over the shallow water for distinct points first. Many times, since the lake is shallow, the land surrounding it is fairly flat and the points are not as noticeable as on a deeper lake. There is always a point where a tributary enters the lake.

Wade in off the point and slowly work your way into deeper water. Spray your casts in all directions and move slowly along the ridge of the sloping underwater point until you find a breakline. Work all points, starting at the upper end of the lake where the water is generally not as clear. An alternative would be to fish the points on the windward side nearest the dam.

Shallow reservoirs can be weedy and may have some sort of a weedline. Hit the weedline points before looking at any other portion of the weeds. After that, forget working the entire weedline, and just look at the shore. Many times, the shoreline can give you a good indication of a prime area to search for structure, while the weeds in the lake just all look alike.

The shoreline structure can often define the prime areas underneath that may be productive bass haunts. Impoundment waters usually offer the maximum in submerged structure.

SUBMERGED STRUCTURE

Scan the lake for submerged ridges or islands. Many times, a weed growth, tree line, or row of fence posts can give away the presence of this island or ridge. Wade both sides and establish contours along the entire ridge. Find the best breakline along this ridge and mark it on your map. The edges of the dropoff closest to deep water should be the most productive.

These areas can be a utopia in a shallow reservoir, and should be explored thoroughly. Bass use them to move along and to hide from their predators. The scattered light in these areas is what all fish prefer.

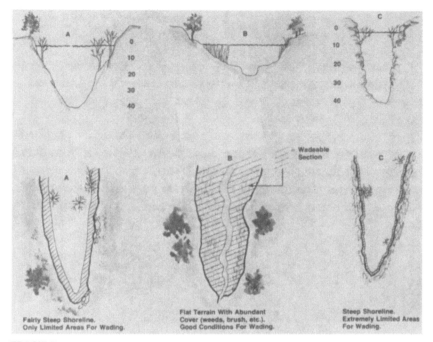

FIGURE 4 — *Reservoirs come in all shapes. A fun way to fish the shallow coves is by wading, but the angler must be very careful in selecting the right one. Surface characteristics can be a tip off to the presence of wadeable areas.*

The most productive reservoir areas for largemouth bass in submerged brush and trees are on any points or in the bushiest trees. The outside edge contour should be mapped first and then work inward. If you are wading and fishing, take care not to step on the brush or trees. Snapping off limbs while you stomp through the area can scatter the bass.

Many times, you'll literally stumble onto super structure while wading standing timber. Many submerged stumps can exist in certain areas and hold bass. The outer edge of the shallow water timber should be productive, since it should exist in deeper water. Again, note depths where action is encountered.

53

Once you have "read" the lake, covered all likely-looking areas and plotted their contours on your structure map, then you are ready to cover "open" water. This can be tiring, but sometimes well worth the effort.

Several holes may exist in the open areas on shallow impoundments and contain many bass. When you find a hole, check out the depth thoroughly (after fishing it) and try to locate a drop-off with underwater structure in it. All holes are potentially productive in shallow reservoirs since dissolved oxygen can penetrate most depths.

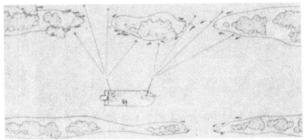

FIGURE 5 — *Reservoir bass in cooler weather are often island-acclimated. Prime areas are the points on windward sides. Forage will move through the cuts and around the shallow points and bass will be waiting.*

TYPICAL PATTERNS CHART

	DEC	JAN	FEB	MAR
Average Water Temperature	65°F	61°F	62°F	70°F
Location	Islands, shore-line weeds near deep water	Humps, dense vegetation, rock piles	Humps, dense vegetation, rock piles	Dense vegetation near deep water, islands
Bait	Crankbaits, worms, spinner baits	Jiggin' spoons, worms, tail spinners, cranks	Worms, spoons, crankbaits	Swimmin' worm, slab baits, cranks
Presentation	Work cuts between land strips at moderate retrieve rates. Hop worms and crank lures.	Jig the spoons on humps and off to the side. Work other baits very slow. Work tail spinners like a worm.	Work cranks slow. Drag worms along the drops and jig the heavy spoons.	Steady retrieve over weeds and along shoreline vegetation.

54

When it's cold with a clear sky, start on the windward side of a reservoir where the dissolved oxygen is high. Try to remember direction of the prevailing wind from the day before and head toward the windward shore. Most heavy vegetation holds heat, and this makes such areas very productive.

Shallow structure on the windward side of any reservoir is always an important area to check out. Waves push forage into the thin-water spots and disguise the presence of an angler.

I've caught bass in 2 to 2 1/2 feet of water on the windward side of a lake. Fish can't feed too much in cold water because their metabolism won't allow it, but the temperature may vary from one side to the other of a reservoir by as much as 10 to 15 degrees.

Once you have plotted all contour lines on the shallow water you fish, you'll have a valuable tool to be used for all seasons! Shallow waters are less predictable than the deeper lakes when weather changes, but they are not impossible. With your new contour map, you can usually eliminate several fishless areas.

On a shallow lake, a contour map is just as important as one on a deeper reservoir. Structure exists on shallow waters also and holds as many fish as the deeper water structure. It's not as near the center of the earth, but it's all relative.

CHAPTER 5

PIT DIGGINGS

Hot Action From Unique Man-Made Waters

THOUSANDS OF WATERCRAFT are car-topped and trailered to numerous man-made bass waters. Lightweight rigs are particularly suited for the pits which seldom have a launch ramp. A trolling motor is generally sufficient to maneuver.

Man-made waters such as mined and borrow pits are abundant in many areas, yet they receive little attention. Irrigation canals, borrow pits dug for highway fill, and even small reservoirs frequently provide great shallow-water bass fishing. An angler can often double his catch-rate in such waters. Bass seem to grow faster and chunkier.

Such waters often get "stocked" naturally. Many yield bass, and most are overlooked. These waters can look ugly yet be full of largemouth. I like to fish places like this due to the lack of angling pressure. I've often found hungry fish and, if I were keeping them, a quick limit.

Most pits have an irregular shoreline. Waters are of medium clarity, but occasionally, a pit can be found with fairly clear water. Many have rocks, sand, and gravel outcroppings along their bottoms.

Bass quickly become adapted to unique pit structures. Brush structure is usually abundant along the lake bottom, and ordinarily, vegetation grows profusely before a pit is flooded. Once inundated, the vegetation provides excellent cover for the entire food chain, from phytoplankton right on up to the largemouth bass.

Lunker hunters concentrate on this terrain to harvest big bass. Many pits in the south have produced bass over 13 or 14 pounds, but seldom does the word get out as to which pit produced the lunker. The lucky anglers are usually pretty tight-lipped about that.

Mining Treasures

Most pits are a result of a mining operation. Thousands of miniature bass factories have been created after rock deposits are enearthed to provide raw material for various end products. In Florida, for example, most of the fabulous phosphate pit fishing occurs in Polk County which lies between Tampa and Orlando. Many pits also exist throughout other states.

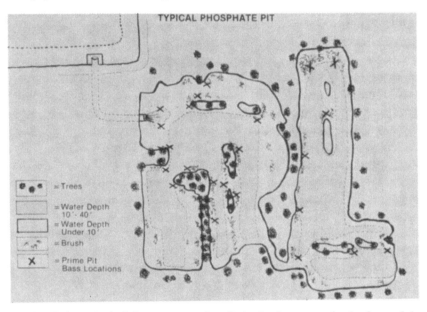

FIGURE 6 — *A pit-fisherman can often find mined treasure in the form of the largemouth bass. Some of the spots with the most potential for holding fish in a typical pit are marked with x's. Those areas are often near heavy cover in shallow water that borders relatively-deeper depths.*

Whereas the phosphate industry was openly criticized several years back for "scarring" the landscape, it now enjoys a reconstructed reputation. The large mining and processing firms are now leaders in creating new bass waters and restoring those pits that have been dug.

Mining companies are following stringent government regulations as they reclaim the land. Nature does its share of the work to green up the shoreline and existing islands, creating excellent habitat for the food chain that normally blossoms in the highly enriched waters. Many of them are stocked, while others prosper due to the wading bird transferral method (eggs on the feet picked up in one pond and loosened in a second, newly-created pit).

STRUCTURE GALORE

When huge dragline buckets are digging through soil to get to the rock beneath, they often create dead end channels and islands and a multitude of structure and depth changes. The massive buckets can take a single scoop of earth, leaving a hole large enough for a 3-bedroom house. The depth of these waters varies from site to site, but our focus is on the shallows.

When the mining operation ceases, the holes are filled with water. Its clarity will vary depending on shoreline characteristics, the drainage land, and the degree of water manipulation (if any) through the pits. The lakes that remain contain underwater humps and other projections above the water surface.

The bass pits in most states vary from a couple of acres up to 500 or so. All of the pits have different structure present. Some have vast pad beds, others cattails and bullrushes, and still others are nearly devoid of emergent vegetation. Some of the better pits even have a profuse growth of hydrilla. Many have sharp dropoffs near some banks while other pits have small hills on the perimeter.

There may be a thousand different types of shoreline on little man-made waters, but the better ones have deep water nearby and some structural characteristics for the bass to migrate along to the shallow bank. The vegetation just off deep water is a good place to begin a search for bass.

Trolling shallow pit structures is a highly effective method for catching big bass during cool periods, as the author's parents found out. The two fish pushing 14 pounds in total were "cranked" out of hydrilla cover on two quick passes.

The forage is often shallow in pits and the predators will move to them. Big bass will bury themselves in the heavy cover and await their prey. Bluegill, golden shiners, shad and other baitfish species are present in most pits throughout the south. Pit bass generally prefer the thin-shaped shad or shiner forage, if available. A popular treat for hungry largemouth is also the crayfish which frequent the numerous rocks found in most pits.

Water levels do vary on many pits connected to a chain of lakes. Control structures often exist to regulate water levels, and the spillways and culverts with flowage are hot spots for feeding bass. The bottom is generally carved out beneath such discharges, and hungry largemouth often lie off to the side of the fast water in four to six foot depths, facing the current.

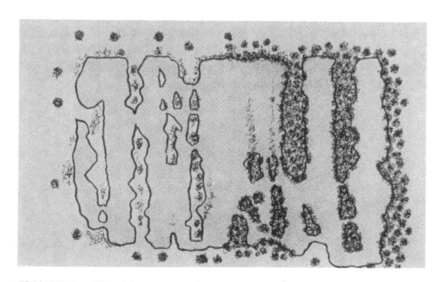

FIGURE 7 — *The older portions of a mined lake, as noted by the more abundant vegetation along the shallows, usually hold far more bass than the cleaner, more recently dug out portions. If the digging looks fresh with very little old vegetation along the bank, look for an area with more profuse cover.*

Strips of submerged "islands" are excellent places for the bass to corner the hapless prey. "Cuts" in the islands are excellent spots to fish since the largemouth generally lay off such areas awaiting a school of bait fish.

Wintertime lure presentations should be slow, as bass are somewhat sluggish. The real heavyweights come from the thick cover or off submerged structure on such retrieves. They will often be in stuff so thick that they have just a small view out. Submerged brush and rock provide a sanctuary to many lunker pit bass.

I'll usually fish any pit shoreline habitat or offshore shallow cover with crankbaits or plastic worms; then I'll look at any depth changes which often require some investigation. If I'm without a depth finder, a tail-spinner lure or 3/8 ounce slip sinker in front of a worm will enable me to figure out depths and changes in depth. Crankbaits that run to 7 or 8 feet are adequate for doing similar evaluation of the bottom terrain.

61

My normal six-hour fishing day on a pit usually results in ten to fifteen bass, which is well above my average production on most other types of water. In Florida, the Game and Fresh Water Fish Commission has verified through creel samplings that pit fishing is more productive than fishing natural lakes, on a fish-per-hour basis. More bass swim in the reclaimed diggings.

Pit fishing is more productive in general than angling in manu other types of water. If the pH is right, bank-bound anglers can get in on the action.

PIT pH FACTORS

When the first pH meter came out several years ago, I quickly learned its value, particularly on phosphate pits. My pH meter read 6.5 at the upper end of the pit near a crude, dirt launch ramp. The water was only 20 inches deep or so for more than a quarter of a mile until I moved through a bend where several islands stood guard on a major portion of the machine-dug bass water.

The bottom dropped to six feet before I felt a need to toss a lure to the heavy cover growing at the pit's edge or around the attractive mid-lake lands. The pH reading was at 6.7 when I hooked my first bass. The following hours were slow though, with only two bass jumping at my crankbaits retrieved through a small stretch of muddy water. In that area, the pH meter indicated a value of 6.8, the closest yet to the 7.5 to 7.9 reading considered "optimal" for feeding largemouth.

Finally, I had another strike and put the three pounder in the boat's aerated well. The pH meter read 7.0. That's a long way from 7.5 but, on that pit, it was the closest that I had seen. And I had covered most of it. Could such a small difference in pH values make a difference in catch rate? It didn't take long to find out. Four casts later, I had two chunky bass in the boat, all from the island and the 7.0 pH water.

HIGH pH LEVELS

The experiment continued in another phosphate pit some four miles down the road. The 40-acre lake was open with no islands or heavy cover along its shore to slow down a strengthening wind.

I began casting the shallow water and let the wind push the boat. After 20 minutes of fruitless casting, the depth dropped to five feet. The pH level was 8.0 when the first largemouth from this pit hit a 7-inch blue worm. For the next 200 yards the action was non-stop until the windward shore shallowed up and the action dwindled back to nothing. The pH kept climbing to a high mark of 8.4 in the final 100 yards of the float.

If two areas offer equal cover and food sources, bass will be found in the areas where the pH is closest to the optimum level. Habitat in the shallows is extremely important too.

I slowly motored back to the beginning of the deep water, where the meter read 8.0, and began another pass. Several chunky bass again put a strain on my rod. Two more passes and sixteen bass caught and released allowed me time to check the other shoreline. I had drifted from the lee to the windward banks along one shoreline only.

I made two passes over the deep water on the other side, working shoreline identical to that across the lake. I was without a single strike but had learned something; the pH reading "shot" up to 8.9 in the apparently barren water. I returned to the opposite bank for a final drift and caught four more keeper-size bass.

Whereas the pH level in the first pit that I fished was uniformly below the 7.5 to 7.9 figure, the waters in the second pit had a range of 8.0 to 8.9. The closer the pH to the preferred range, the better would be the bass angling.

The pH factor in shallow water is likely to change drastically during the course of a day. Photosynthesis by green plants causes the pH of water to go higher. Factors will alter it on cloudy days and after the sun goes down. For bass, look for water with good habitat that is closest to pH 7.5 to 7.9, whether it is above or below this range!

Pit bass are active year around. Water temperatures are usually conducive to feeding fish, which makes the angling easier. Man-dug waters provide a variety of cover, and the hot action can generally be found angling from a small boat or by casting from bank side.

CHAPTER 6

RIVERS, CREEKS, AND RUN-INS

MOVING WATER AND MIGRATING BASS

SHALLOW RIVERS and creeks throughout the country have received an unfair reputation as being sparsely populated, small bass waters. Many heavyweights do exist in tributaries of all sizes though, and productive methods unique to these waterways can aid an angler's catch in terms of quality and quantity.

Successful angling concepts on natural lakes and reservoirs won't always work on an environment, part of which is constantly in motion. Current dictates a slightly different approach to finding and catching the largemouth bass. Habitat orientation and bait or lure presentation take on significant meaning in moving waters. Consideration of each is vital to the successful river angler.

River systems throughout the country are finally beginning to generate some interest among the bass fishing fraternity. The St. Lawrence River (NY), Arkansas River (AR), Alabama River (AL) and Kissimmee River (FL) have all achieved a modicum of publicity resulting from their production of some significant catches for both weekend and tournament anglers.

In Florida alone there are approximately 1,700 streams. They range in size from small spring creeks to large rivers. Undoubtedly, more big largemouth bass are in the 318-mile long St. Johns River than in any other. However, highly productive big bass waters exist in thousands of other lesser-known rivers and creeks throughout the country.

While some tributaries harbor bass that seldom see a lure, others seem to keep their legacy of great bass angling a secret. Specific techniques that produce in current conditions on one river will often work well on others, but successful fishermen must learn to "read" the water and adapt their angling to the specific waterway.

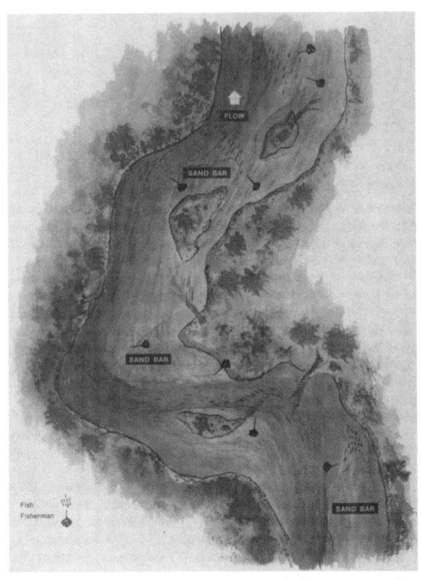

FIGURE 8 — *Rivers can offer a great bass fishery. Shallow streams even have ample depth for certain species of bass and many are very wadeable. Try to pick out the prime river bass areas.*

Some rivers are comprised of demineralized, nutrient-poor waters, usually exhibiting little evidence of biological productivity of fish and plants, however many are chemically suited for a great bass fishery. Often, these rivers support very active populations of shallow largemouth that are relatively undisturbed by anglers.

FOOD CHAIN

One of the keys in putting river bass in the boat lies in knowing the predominant forage available to the top predator fish. The variety is different from that found in a natural lake or reservoir. Concentrations of favorite impoundment forage such as the threadfin shad are seldom found in the smaller tributaries of the south. They are completely non-existent in northern rivers. Other species, likewise, may be present in some waters and not in others.

Rivers and creeks generally have a smaller food chain than is found in the large lakes. While crappie, for example, is usually found in lesser quantities, other sunfish are found in greater numbers by percent of the overall forage base. Shiners and other smaller minnow species may be found in greater numbers. Naturally, the crayfish is more numerous in the rocky, sandy reaches of smaller tributaries than in mud-bottom lake waters.

Moving waters dictate specific lure selections that closely resemble the particular forage frequently found in rivers and creeks. Jigs, spinners, small crankbaits, short plastic worms, and rubber crayfish imitations are generally more productive. From observation, stomach analysis, discussions with local fisheries biologists or other anglers, try to determine the forage most available in that particular river and then match the lure action, shape, and coloration to it. Weedless baits that are less prone to being swept into a permanent position under a rocky crevice are more practical here.

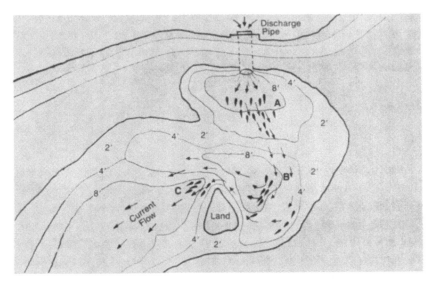

FIGURE 9 — *Moving water can occur at a variety of locations. If the current is not too heavy, bass will usually be in position A. If the current intensity increases, we can expect the bass to move out and relocate at position B. When the current is really blowing out, the bass will commonly be found in spots similar to position C — a great ambush point.*

Lures that are more controllable in currents are usually more productive. In some river situations, currents limit unanchored craft to a fairly rapid float trip offering only one cast per fish-holding structure. The successful angler must consider all that, and even more, in his lure selection.

CURRENT CONSIDERATIONS

An angler who is better able to handle a smaller area with better defined casting targets must also cope with the moving water. While fish in shallow rivers are often more concentrated, only a lure presented in near proximity to them will work. The cast must account for a movement imparted by the current, in addition to that "inspired" by the angler.

70

Bass will usually "hug" the obstacles, bottom, or sides of a body of moving water. Place your lure in the shallow rapids, riffles, or other areas of rapid current, and you may catch a spotted, Guadalupe, redeye, shoal, Suwannee, or smallmouth bass, depending on which state and waters you're fishing. For the ever-popular largemouth, however, any area of diminished current is a potential ambush point.

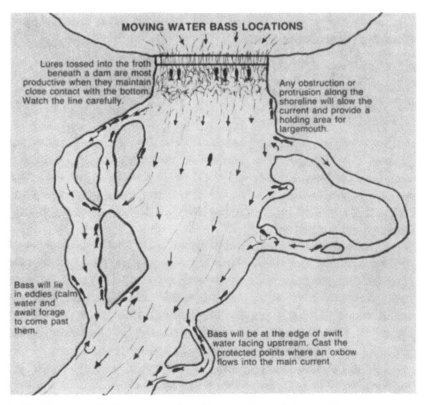

FIGURE 10 — *Shallow tributaries off reservoirs and rivers offer great areas to sneak up on bass. Lure selection and presentation are particularly important in such areas.*

71

Current is slowed by "bends" in the river or creek. A good bass stream usually has several bends of various configurations that collect structure, such as fallen trees and brush. Eddies behind the submerged structure act as those adjacent to high velocity current in bends. Backwaters, or eddies, attract largemouth and aid them in their foraging activity. For this reason, bends are extremely productive areas on most tributaries. They just seem to "collect" bass.

Bends also create a variance in the depth of the channel, which is conducive to big bass habitation. The flow gouges out the bottom and outer bank, and a deeper than normal depth results, in addition to a quick dropping shore. Wooden debris piling up at these bends is often the only structure found.

TRIBUTARY TRIUMPH

I was recently fishing a reservoir with little luck when I decided to move to a tributary. The depth at the creek's entrance was a mere two feet, and I had to keep my bass rig on a plane to cut across the blockage of heavy vegetation. Having enough momentum to break through the weed barrier was the key to discovering the great bass fishing on the other side.

Once beyond the clogged passageway, the creek waters of five to six foot depths meandered through lily pads towards the nearby forest. Soon, cypress and oak trees bordered the small stream and cast shadows over much of the water. In two short hours of midmorning fishing, I caught nine largemouth bass in some of the fastest fishing I've ever had. The bass ranged in size from one to about four pounds, and the action never ceased.

I found two distinct patterns. First, the holes gouged out to 7 foot depths by heavy current where the creek made almost 90-degree turns or "necked" down in tight narrow runs where productive areas. The largemouth would be positioned in the slower water below and to the side of the fast current.

The second prime location was on the submerged brush in the outer bends of the small stream. Those bends were relatively deeper than the runs, and tree limbs in that area drew bass like a magnet.

I was able to attract at least one largemouth from each similar area with small, 4 and 6 inch plastic worms. The bait was cast to a bluff bank and "crawled" into the stream and down the drop where a bass was often waiting. While there were no real lunkers among the enticed, the average size of bass on the bends was impressive.

River bends are very productive, particularly those with excellent shoreline cover. They often collect submerged brush and lunker largemouth.

Overhanging trees, fallen branches, and totally submerged brush can offer river largemouth a shallow, protected home with plenty of food. Such terrain also provides excellent shade which seems to be more important for the bass of a shallow river system versus those in a deep lake.

Indentations are often inhabited by king-size bass. The small inlet out of the main current provides predators with a point for ambush. Smart "river rats" will cast to such spots.

The shoreline cover's relation to the sun should always be a consideration. The smart angler will use it in conjunction with the bank cover for best results. In the winter, I'll fish the sun-warmed shore first since it may be a degree or two warmer. Direct rays on that bank may also attract some forage from hiding to bask in the sun.

Indentations in the shoreline may denote the presence of a run-in or the intersection of two creeks. Excellent structure in the form of a steep-sided underwater point is often created when a small stream or run-in converges with a river. Often a drop is formed in this area, and that's worth several casts. Bass usually lie in the slower moving current near the confluence, waiting for food to swim by.

PRIME TARGETS

The exposed roots of a submerged tree adjacent to deeper water are attractive to baitfish and bass. Likewise, casting to overhanging brush where bugs, grasshoppers, worms, and other morsels periodically fall into the water, is productive. Submerged timber will create an eddy on one side as water is channeled around the obstruction. Cast into this backwash where bass await their supper.

Submerged logs provide cover for small minnows and bass. Cast parallel to and near the structure. Points jutting into the water and sloughs off a main channel are excellent targets for the lure tosser. In muddy or off-color water, the angler can work the well-defined targets closer and fine-tune his casting and presentation. Smaller tributaries may be clearer after sustained high winds, requiring use of small lures and light lines, or they may be more roily after a thunderstorm, allowing use of larger gator-tail worms and baitcasting gear.

While stained water is easy to flip with a swinging, underhand cast, most of the successful river anglers use pinpoint casts of 15 to 25 feet. Naturally, on a creek barely wider than the boat, the fisherman should pick targets in front of him. Some of the smallest flows offer the best spring bass angling opportunities to jig-and-worm tossers. Sand bars and shallow flats are prime spots to fish at this time.

Successful river angling requires the ability to "read" the unique topography, to determine an appropriate lure based on forage availability and current parameters, and to present that bait correctly to the bass. Fishermen may have a challenging trek to discover the better opportunities, but they will be there. Fortunately for us "river rats", productive exploration of the river bass fishery remains pretty much an isolated incident.

WATER CLARITY

Some states are blessed with large deposits of limestone which contribute to a network of underground and above-ground river systems. Calm, pristine waterways meander through pastures and swamps. Many are crystal clear, yet harbor multitudes of bass which have seldom seen a fisherman's lure.

Spring-fed waters produce a variety of bass, like the author's 2 1/2 pound Suwannee bass. Even river largemouth find the crayfish an important part of their diet. A plug resembling the crustacean will produce!

76

Clear water generally isn't as nutrient-rich, therefore, it does not afford a food base conducive to large bass growth. Under normal circumstances, a maximum weight of 10 to 12 pounds is achievable for bass in spring-fed waters. Tannic acid stain and other influences, as well as depth of the water, contribute to maximum growth in the largemouth.

Calcareous waters dictate a food chain somewhat unique to bass territories. Stomach content analysis by fishery biologists has revealed that up to 90% of the food intake of the stream bass can be crayfish. This factor can aid an angler in determining the appropriate lures and bait to use. Brown and red colored plastic worms are ideal, as are the many plastic crayfish imitations. Small spinners and spoons directly imitate the smaller fish forage on which the largemouth often feeds.

An enterprising angler can create his own bass catching spots. When running tributaries, position the boat near shore so that the wake will stir up the water adjacent to the shoreline. The disturbance will also knock small forage into the water, and bass will soon be moving along the area to feed. Turn the boat around and then fish the banks with the stained water.

During the late spring, when rivers are full and draining into lakes, the pH levels near the mouth of such tributaries are often drastically changed. Such areas are highly visible when the runoff is muddy water and the lake is relatively clear water. In general, late spring brings more fluctuation of pH levels, which can even change hour to hour.

Fall brings the decay of fallen leaves and other plants, decreasing water clarity and pH levels. River fish move shallower then as their "ideal" pH range rises. When aquatic plants begin to go dormant for the winter, the pH level in the creeks and tributaries will be affected first and start its downward trend.

CHAPTER 7

TIDE WATERS

WHERE SALT AND FRESH WATER MINGLE

IT IS NOT UNUSUAL to see limited boat traffic in brackish tributaries, even near major population centers. The majority of fresh water anglers are attracted to inland reservoirs, natural lakes, and rivers. Seldom are they even knowledgeable about the tidal effects on coastal bass and, for that reason, estuary waters with excellent bass fishing are often overlooked.

Thousands of miles of tidal tributaries stretch along the Gulf coast around the Florida peninsula and up the Atlantic coast. The productivity of these brackish waters is more consistent and often surpasses that of inland waters. The estuaries are teeming with largemouth bass forage such as fingerlings of both fresh and salt water fish, shrimp, crabs, snails and salamanders.

While hungry bass may be as numerous as their forage, an understanding of tidal influences is vital for angler success. Barometric pressure affects tides on the earth's surface. Bodies of water are moved about, causing changes in water level, temperature, and clarity. Tides dry up shoreline habitat during low periods as they sweep estuary forage along in their current.

Bass fishermen have long known that barometric pressure can affect the fishing, but few realize this is the major parameter in tidal action. Barometric pressure affecting the tides on the earth's surface is established primarily by the moon's orbit. This pressure forces a large body of water downward in one area, creating a low tide at that particular place, while elsewhere on the area's perimeter, the water level will rise slightly.

79

An undiscovered fishery exists in most tidal waters. Many giant largemouth swim the brackish currents and feed on shrimp, crabs, and other "unusual" forage.

The moon circles the earth in an elliptical orbit every 28 days. Its gravitational pull on the earth's seas is not uniform. The sun, to a lesser extent, has some gravitational pull also, and these parameters along with others go into making the tide tables that can be found in coastal areas.

TIDE TIMING

Without going into a lot of detail, tides can be categorized as either spring tides or neap tides, and are related to the phases of the moon. Gravitational pull of the water is highest (spring tide) when the moon is closest to the earth and in line with the sun. A spring tide occurs every two weeks in most areas, during the new and full moon phases, and has the highest high tides and the lowest low tides of the four week period. Less rise and fall is seen on the neap tide, which usually occurs on the first and third quarter moon phases. The angler can remember to check the moon to determine the tidal phase the night before his fishing trip.

Tides vary depending on the moon phase and other factors. Figuring out the coastal estuaries and tide tables will pay big dividends. Catch a tide right and catch a bass right.

81

Tides repeat themselves about every 14 days, and they occur approximately one hour later each day. The tide tables list the depths of the water at coastal locations as mean, or average, low tide. While the level can be lower, few anglers realize that the tide still flows after the lowest (or highest) point of the tide.

Correlating the tables to our favorite fishing spots in tidal waters from the nearest reference station is extremely difficult. The tide delay depends on several factors, such as depth, width, fresh water discharge, wind, rain, runoff, etc., so actual observation is the best way to determine this factor. Once this time differential is established for a particular area in the river, tides could be predictable under future normal conditions. From the tide tables, then, the selection of the optimum times to be pursuing bass can be made days ahead of time.

On falling tides, the baitfish are forced from their hideouts into the main channel, and the fast flowing water sweeps the weaker swimmers towards their predators. This is why the falling tide is, in general, the most productive phase of tidal bass fishing. Rising tides can open up shorelines and flats for fish to feed, resulting in some good fishing if one hits it right. The slow time in brackish water bass fishing is the time lapse between the change of tides.

After the lull during slack tide, bass proceed to feed on the incoming tidal currents with somewhat less vigor. At high tide, when the marshy flats are flooded, top water plugs and small spinners will occasionally entice feeders from the grass. Feeding activity again slows near high slack tide, and generally remains slow until the tide falls rapidly.

SALTY CONSIDERATIONS

Since a falling tide is generally better, most anglers plan on launching their boats at dead high tide (slack). They'll then normally have about 4 or 5 hours of outgoing tide before a turn around in flow, and many times, in bass activity.

Much of the cover in a tidal plain exists in shallow waters. When the tide is out, the shoreline cover is high and dry. Concentrate your angling around the first shallow drop a few feet from shore.

Although current has the biggest influence on bass feeding activity day in and day out, wind, cold fronts, and muddy water can alter the movements substantially. This is especially true during neap tide, when water level changes are minimal. Winds can accelerate, or sometimes (although rare) even reverse tidal current flow, and at these times the feeding is unpredictable.

Deep water structure is seldom found in these waters. Very little submerged brush exists on the marsh flat areas of the rivers and creeks, but the shallow marsh grass at the bank is thick and rugged.

The creek bends in the wooded sections contain brush piles near the bank, and occasional fallen trees dot the shoreline in those areas.

Barnacles in brackish waters are a presence to deal with, and break-offs are common when there are docks, piers, or even logs. Many tidal rivers and their tributaries contain submerged brush that is coated with the saltwater crustacean, so beware.

Both barnacles and crabs can give an angler fits while he is trying to worm his way to some good bass. The crabs will quickly grab a plastic worm, and the angler will set the hook, thinking a bass has it. Then, when a bass grabs the next presentation and goes around a tree limb, slicing the line on the hook set, the angler is too offguard to yank him away from the knife-like barnacles. Anglers a couple of miles up any of the creeks are less prone to such "salty" harassment.

Flood waters and severe changes in weather can also lessen the certainty of a nice stringer of tidal bass. Heavy rains can lower the salinity of shallow brackish water and force fish towards the sea, while a drought or long dry season can result in greater salt water intrusion, moving the bass upstream. This does depend a great deal, however, on the flowage rates of the tributaries. As salinity increases, bass find their tolerance for brackish water waning, so it's important to know how salty the water might be.

As the water freshens and becomes tolerable for acclimated bass, the plant life takes on a slightly different character. Noting the presence of aquatic plants near the shoreline is one way of determining where the brackish water begins on the river. Lily pads and water hyacinths show up much more often in the fresher water, since both have low resistance to high salt content. Numerous arrowhead and elephant ear plants denote fresh enough waters for the largemouth.

Prime Locations

Bass will generally find the fresher waters. Cuts where shallow areas run into tidal rivers are prime spots. These run-ins congregate baitfish, and bass will often be there during an outgoing tide. The same tide will leave fallen weeds along the bank and mud flats. Largemouth can often be found on the quick drops just off the shallow flats, which give them a choice of depth or vegetation cover.

There are plenty of logs, stumps, and eddy areas in most tidal rivers. The river changes though, from one tide to the next. Outer bends may be consistent on either tide, but the nature of the run just above and below it determines the current speed on each tidal phase. A sharp bend immediately in front of another bend, for example, would slow the current action, while a long straight run would allow it to move faster.

Tidal action in the tributaries varies from coast to coast. Brackish waters on the east coast experience two high and two low tides each day, while tributaries on the Gulf side generally experience only one high and one low tide. The farther west an angler goes, the more difficult it is for him to detect any tidal action.

Once a pattern has been established and bass are taken, these brackish waters should be fished back and forth along the productive area. On several jaunts to a tidal bassin' hole, my partner and I have often taken a dozen bass from a single creek bend.

Plastic worms, particularly the salt-impregnated kind, fool their share of bass in the tidal river bends. When the tide falls so much that shoreline structure lies exposed, floating balsa lures retrieved across the shallow flats can account for largemouth bass. As the tide continues to fall, successful anglers switch back to worms to probe the river bends.

Tidewater Bass Locations

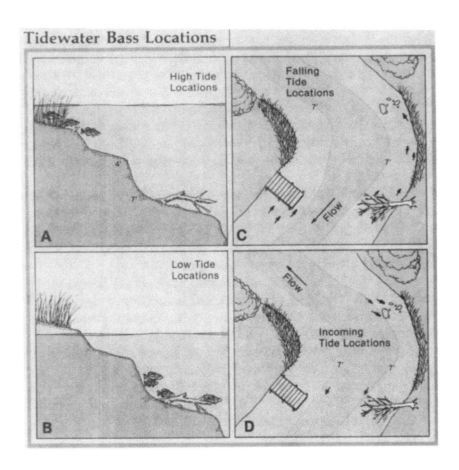

SOUTHERN TIDEWATERS

Florida's St. Johns River, near its entrance to the Atlantic Ocean at Jacksonville, is covered with bass-filled piers and pilings, which are coated with saltwater crustaceans and knife-like barnacle growth. The docks attract big bass during the hot months. While my largest from these waters was just shy of ten pounds, several over that mark are usually caught each month of the year in the area. All four major St. Johns' tributaries near its mouth are often overlooked as being "saltwater", yet they contain superb bass fishing.

FLORIDA TIDAL BASS RIVERS

1. Perdido River
2. Choctawhatchee River
3. Apalachicola River
4. Ochlockonee River
5. St. Marks River
6. Aucilla River
7. Suwanee River
8. Wacasassa River
9. Withlacoochee River
10. Crystal River
11. Homosassa River
12. Chassahowitzka River
13. Braden River
14. Myakka River
15. Peace River
16. St. Lucie River
17. Tomoka River
18. St. Johns River
19. Nassau River
20. St. Mary's River

FIGURE 12 — *Florida has more tidal bass water than any other state. Shallow, river delta systems are more prevalent on the Gulf than along the Atlantic, but the largemouth fishing is exceptional along both coasts.*

River delta systems are more prevalent on the Gulf than along the Atlantic. The Apalachicola River is a good example of brackish water discharge into bays. The numerous bayous, sloughs, and small, hidden waterways just off Apalachicola Bay are full of healthy largemouth bass.

On a trip to that river, I was casting worms in some of the muddiest water I've seen, with quite good results. After only two hours of fishing, I had seven largemouth. A one-pound bluegill leaped on the surface ahead of our boat. I felt the small fish was "forage" in this instance, and was probably being chased. Casting a 3-inch topwater plug to the splash of the descending bluegill brought an immediate strike from a 7 pound, 10 ounce largemouth. It was a fine anchor for my stringer that day.

Most shallow tidal areas hold limits of largemouth bass. Those areas with numerous bends are better on the falling tide, while areas composed primarily of long runs between each bend are more productive on an incoming tide. Delta waters along the seaboard have substantial amounts of each.

CHAPTER 8

LARSEN'S "FLORA FACTOR"

ANALYZING SHALLOW WATER SYSTEMS

THE MOST IMPORTANT KNOWLEDGE any bass angler can acquire is the ability to "read the water" and locate his quarry. This analysis often takes years of on-the-water experience. Data to base it on is sometimes compiled slowly.

Larsen's "Flora Factor" is a carefully developed, analytical technique to figure out optimal bass locations in a body of water. It is based primarily on vegetation and its relationship to a healthy fishery. An analysis of the interface that reveals where to find bass in lakes or rivers is presented herein as a concept.

Theory and reasoning are delineated to aid in complete understanding of this chapter. It's an excellent way to take a comprehensive look at a shallow water system and derive appropriate information. From that, we should catch more bass. Without sounding like a textbook, lets get into the concept and we'll summarize the results, in time.

GENERAL BACKGROUND

The value of vegetation in a healthy, productive fishery is well known. Studies by various states' biologists have shown waters with heavy aquatic plant growth are many times more productive than those with little vegetation!

It wasn't too many years ago that bass benefits from aquatic plants were entirely unknown. Naturally, since some plants' detrimental impact overshadowed any advantages, the latter was

89

seldom, if ever, mentioned. It's true that a few weed types can destroy wildlife habitat, clog up small tributaries, make navigation difficult and speed up the deterioration of a body of water—if they get out of control.

Shallow water cover, like cattails, holds nice bass year-round. Not all emergent vegetation is productive and knowing the differences is important.

Emergent vegetation, like cattails, can spread by an underground root system as well as by seeds, but it is fairly easy to control. Filamentous algae (growing in long strands), on the other hand, plagues anglers and boaters and can be difficult to control. Phytoplankton (suspended microscopic algae) is usually considered beneficial and a vital link in the basic food chain. Some difficult-to-control submerged weeds, with roots attached to the bottom, can take over an extremely clear lake.

Most weed woes, if you can call them that, began with the introduction of exotic plants over the past 50 years. Hydrilla and others have few natural enemies and can spread quickly. Environmentalists called it an "invasion of water weeds". It's true that an influx of aquatic plants that are not native to an area can drastically impact the ecological balance of the water, but for the most part, vegetation in any form is beneficial to most waters.

The predator bass love it. Food, protection, cover, and ideal water characteristics such as dissolved oxygen and temperature are attractive to the largemouth. The more dense the cover, too, the better for most fisheries. Lily pads, reeds, bullrushes, sawgrass, etc., all have the ability to become thick masses of seemingly impenetrable cover.

Bass will burrow far under such thick growth to find protection from their predators above, ample shade from the sun's rays, and food. They can easily ambush prey from their positions deep in vegetation, and they enjoy forage such as frogs, freshwater shrimp, panfish, minnows, eels, crayfish, and other items from the weed-menu. With the abundance of food in the vegetation-infested areas, there is little doubt why so many bass congregate in it most of their lives.

Aquatic plant life is here to stay in most rivers and lakes, and the angler should learn to analyze that environment. What may appear a nuisance to one angler could be a vital key to another. Knowing what to look for and then correctly fishing that area, can prove that.

THE NUTRIENT KEY

The nutrient level in a lake or river is responsible for aquatic growth, sound water chemistry, and a healthy fishery. High nutrient levels usually mean high populations of bass. Excess nutrients is the real problem in most lakes that are perceived to have a "weed" problem.

Aquatic vegetation has, itself, often been responsible for over-enrichment of waters, causing a progressing state of decay. As stated, control can be a problem on some lakes and streams, but in general, aquatic plant life has received a bad rap.

Aquatic vegetation can over-enrich some waters, but most forms and coverage is only beneficial to a body of water. Understanding Larsen's "Flora Factor" is a beginning to larger bass and more of them.

The proliferation of vegetation in highly-enriched lakes has spawned lists of "preferred" species. While hydrilla and water hyacinths are often thought undesirable, beneficial vegetation on the lists includes pickerel weed, arrowhead, eel grass, chara, and pond weed. In moderation, bullrushes, lily pads, and cattails are considered very beneficial to a body of water. Regardless of species type, waters with an abundance of vegetation almost always have a large population of forage and game fish.

Nutrient levels can be determined by several things. In addition to the prolific vegetation growth, the water color can also reveal the better spots to fish. Waters with excessive nutrients have a green or brown tint to them. If they are too fertile, algae mats will probably be present. If the water is muddy, there is little chance that the lake is too fertile. The turbidity shuts out the rays of sunlight which are necessary for growth of the microscopic plants.

Vegetation growth is highly dependent on sunlight and is, of course, more prominent in shallow areas. Any problems are more severe in clear (and wind-protected) water, since sunlight penetrates to a greater depth. Ideally productive waters will be composed of a balance of shallow (less than four feet) and deeper areas. They will have a clarity of one to three feet (maximum).

Look closely at any crops or land-based vegetation in the drainage area of any body of water. If they are poor, so should the fish crop be. If you notice poor wheat, corn, etc., that should reveal that the soil is not fertile enough (low nutrient level) either for the crops or for sustaining any number of good sized bass. Usually, the more "uncultivated" the drainage area, the better the fishing will be.

TOPOGRAPHY ANALYSIS

One key in finding good concentrations of bass is to determine the type of brush present. Knowing the types of trees will often clue an angler to the approximate depth of water. Willow trees, for example, seem to "pop up" around a water hole. Cypress and some hardwoods grow in low areas, while pine tree stands grow on higher (and dryer) land. In a new reservoir with both types inundated, the shallower water will be covering the pine and the cypress should be in the deep stuff.

Tree-lined banks are usually on higher ground, denoting deeper channels beneath their root system. Low marshy areas of sandy soil seldom sustain large trees or provide quick drops. Large living trees on a bank are usually a good indication of stable water conditions. Firmer bottoms and sharper dropoffs at that point can usually be expected. Swampy shorelines have water levels which often fluctuate and do not allow most types of large trees to thrive.

Finding bass feeding in certain areas of vegetation can be a memorable experience. Try to ascertain "why" though and remember that. Bottom characteristics may be different or a slight depth change may be present.

Certain types of weeds and grasses can be associated with different bottom characteristics. Some aquatic plants thrive in soft mud (or muck) where bass seldom take up residence, but most others grow on firmer sandy or marl bottoms, which provide great fish habitat. The bottom can often change depending on where you are in a lake, so the smart angler will check out all of it. Bullrushes, for example, may prosper in the sandy soil on one side of a body of

94

water, yet the opposite shore could reflect little in the way of desirable vegetation.

I've often found that stretches of brushy banks held good fish only, and that extremely shallow marshy stretches seldom held more than one or two yearling largemouth. When moving from one to the other, I noticed the strikes would just stop at a point where very little shoreline cover existed and the sharp breaking banks lost their gradient.

Similarly, high banks indicate adjacent deeper water (relatively); flat banks usually denote shallow depths. Heavy aquatic weed growth which ends abruptly may mean a quick drop in depth, while less dense vegetation which gradually "sinks" below the surface could denote a slow-tapered, shallow bank.

MACRO-ANALYSIS OF INDICATORS

Now, let's look closely at the plant community and try to understand why variations exist.

Photosynthesis is the growth process of all forms of vegetation, including aquatic plants, algae, and microscopic organisms. This chemical reaction occurs primarily in sunlight and has the effect of raising the pH levels of water with heavy vegetation.

Natural lakes in the Sunbelt with mostly shallow water have an obvious increase in pH levels during daylight hours due to the vegetation growth in the lakes' shallow areas. If there is a significant amount of plant and animal life decay on the bottom, however, the pH levels near the bottom will be lower than in the shallows simply because of the acid released from decomposition. A pH meter allows tracking of this parameter and can help find (and cull) areas with poor bottom composition.

Most weed masses will have their thickest stands near shore. Shallow water clarity usually promotes this characteristic, but density and height are dependent on localized soil nutrients as well as water chemistry. Taller groups of vegetation are generally healthier than shorter stands of the same species. They also attract more bass. If certain beds of aquatic plants appear to be doing very well, fish them!

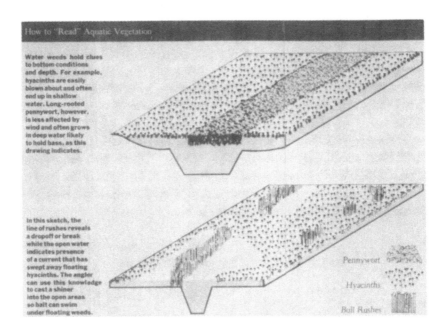

Water weeds hold clues to bottom conditions and depth. For example, hyacinths are easily blown about and often end up in shallow water. Long-rooted pennywort, however, is less affected by wind and often grows in deep water likely to hold bass, as this drawing indicates.

In this sketch, the line of rushes reveals a dropoff or break while the open water indicates presence of a current that has swept away floating hyacinths. The angler can use this knowledge to cast a shiner into the open areas so bait can swim under floating weeds.

Pennywort

Hyacinths

Bull Rushes

FIGURE 13 — *Larsen's "Flora Factor" includes a macro-analysis of vegetative indicators. Correct interpretation of the various parameters should result in more bass.*

The same thing generally occurs with coloration of plants and trees. Those sporting a darker (green) color are either soaking up more nutrients (and are healthier) or they are a variety that reproduces well in the enriched soil. Optimal bottom characteristics support shoreside trees with dark green leaves while less nutritious soils have lighter-green forests nearby. Check out the dark green house plants of a gardener versus those pale ones of a professional angler/outdoor writer.

Shoreline and weedline irregularity enhances productivity of a fishery. The ratio of shoreline length versus surface water acreage is often evaluated by fish management personnel to aid in predicting the production capabilities (pounds per acre base) for new impoundments. Weed points and pockets within a mass of vegetation are used by bass to ambush their forage. The more, the merrier.

Another indicator of healthy vegetation and optimal conditions for bass is reflected in the insect life on the plants. Examine the plant communities for bugs, particularly blind mosquitoes. Aquatic weed patches that attract an influx of insects also are inviting to bass. The relationship between the vegetation and entire food chain is extremely important.

FACTOR SUMMARIZATION

We've considered several components of Larsen's "Flora Factor". Each particular analysis is important to the complete concept. It is a "system" for determining the best place to find largemouth bass. Waters and areas with minimal potential can be quickly "culled" with this approach.

For shallow water patterning, Larsen's "Flora Factor" should be extremely valuable to all bass anglers. Recapping the basic analysis is necessary to develop the complete picture, however, the theory behind each component should be understood for addressing parameter variations while "on the water".

In brief, Larsen's "Flora Factor" consists of a ten-part analysis:

- Determine the nutrient-level of tributaries and watershed from vegetation crops present, and then fish nearest the healthiest (subjective to some extent).

- Identify the bottom composition, verify the extent of decomposition with a pH meter, and then fish the cleanest sandy soil available.

- Determine the tallest, healthiest plant beds of a particular species, and then fish them.

- Scan shoreline trees for a color difference and then fish the area nearest the darker green vegetation.

- Identify water color variances in a lake or stream, and then fish vegetated areas having a 1 to 2-foot visibility.

- Identify the types of inundated trees in a reservoir to determine their approximate elevation prior to impoundment, and then start fishing the largest timber currently in waters between four and seven feet deep.

- Scan the shoreline of a natural lake to find the heaviest concentration of trees at the water's edge, and then fish there.

- Determine bottom topography in and around the vegetation, and fish where there is some relatively deep water access.

- Determine bodies of water or areas within, having very irregular shoreline cover or offshore weedlines, and then concentrate on angling there.

- Check out several weed patches to determine the bug community present, and then fish those that have attracted the most insects.

CHAPTER 9

SUBMERGED VEGETATION

WEEDS BENEATH THE WAVES

A FREQUENT PROBLEM for many anglers is how to properly fish waters with submerged vegetation. But more and more fishermen are figuring out just how to cope with the water weeds and catch largemouth bass.

Many anglers have developed methods to effectively fish such habitat as hydrilla, eel grass, elodea, and coontail moss. Their ways are highly productive, and a limit of big bass is not an uncomfortable goal for most.

Aquatic weed life offers shelter for fish food organisms, shade, and more comfortable water temperatures for light-shy fish. The sediment from aquatic plants can pile up on the lake's bottom if the plants become too populous and begin to die. The bottom sediment warms up the water in the winter though, while the shade from the plant cover cools the water in the summer.

Some submerged plants like elodea and hydrilla may mat up too quickly, robbing the lower levels of the plant from sunlight exposure. This prevents photosynthesis from taking place and depletes the dissolved oxygen in the area. Smart anglers will avoid the really heavy mats of weeds, which are decaying.

In lakes which are full of hydrilla or coontail moss, there will seldom be a feeding migration to the shoreline. The holes in the weeds are ideal for locating big bass.

Hydrilla, which often grows to the water's surface and then mats up, has spread throughout the states. But it provides fish with extraordinary cover. Many anglers are bewildered by the mass of weeds in their favorite waters. Others have found it to be unique, productive structure.

A chemically-sprayed boat lane through hydrilla, representing only an 18-inch depth change will offer a migration route to the bass. In weed-clogged waters such areas often produce huge largemouth.

Chemicals sprayed over hydrilla to make boat lanes will knock the plant down only where sprayed. Then, as the water level rises above the weed mass, there is a "slot" below the majority of the hydrilla. Bass will use these trails to move along because they are one to two feet deeper than the top of the submerged hydrilla. The change may be small and difficult to detect, but finding one is definitely worth it. Dozens of trophy bass have been caught from such structure.

In shallow bodies of water, hydrilla can hinder navigation and obstruct current flow. Fortunately, in most waters, this is not a problem. Where there are no excessive silt deposits nor a high potential for flood damage, the surrounding presence of hydrilla simply provides the best cover in the world for fingerlings to escape predators.

The growth of hydrilla has created new "breaks" and even helped define existing structures, in some cases. A "weed line" may establish the presence of a quick drop in depth due to a creek bed or river channel.

SHAGGY SHALLOWS

Several thousands of acres of "shag carpet" exist in some lakes scattered around the U.S. Hydrilla, a rooted plant, can survive in almost any weather and spread by fragmentation. Small fragments on a boat trailer can be "transplanted" from one lake to another, and from state to state. The fragments then root and grow into large plants, thus infiltrating another lake.

Wind, waves, and boaters cut and separate the soft upper shoots of this competitive plant, which establishes itself firmly. Shade or water clarity has little effect on its growth. It will, however, grow towards the sunlight once it has been established in depths.

Although several lakes and coves of large reservoirs are choked with mats of hydrilla, fishing for bass and most other species improves. What was once a good bass lake is often transformed by hydrilla to a great lake. The plant can become a menace during spawning season if the shallows become clogged, but good spawns have taken place despite seemingly "bad" conditions. The fish population in most lakes with a hydrilla influx actually increases.

TOP WATER WAYS

To attract the bass from deep in the moss bed to the surface requires lures that can disturb the surface in a "natural" manner. Little movement is actually required to disturb a smooth surface and produce some audible noise, because bass in the shade and concealment of the weed bed will usually observe what is going on above them.

Since the action and control of most surface lures is through the rod tip, a taut line is a must for fishing heavy weed cover. Another advantage of surface-worked lures on hydrilla-infested waters is that they bring the bass to the top, making it easier for the angler to keep the largemouth out of the entanglements below. And that is the key to landing them in this cover.

Many experts fish topwater lures along hydrilla beds early in the morning and late in the day. This is very dependent on the wind conditions and time of year though. In the spring, before profuse hydrilla growth hits the surface of some lakes, a clear, top water bait fished over the plant will be productive.

As the summer progresses, bass move back into the moss. Aquatic plants often grow to the surface of lakes and then mat up. Catching bass from hydrilla, coontail moss, and other submerged plants then requires special methods. To be an effective producer in this type of cover, the weedless lure must ride the surface easily.

SPINNERS AND SPOONS

Single-shaft spinners and spoons are very effective in heavy hydrilla cover. A single hook and ability to ride the surface and bounce over small obstructions is the key to the spoon.

In mats of hydrilla and other submerged vegetation, the plastic worm is a weedless way to work deep into the cover. There are a variety of rigs that can be used depending on the density of the weedbed.

The retrieve should begin just before the lure hits the water. The design of the lure dictates how the lure will ride on its way back to the boat. Bass may follow a lure for several feet in the hydrilla-covered waters before pouncing on it. When a second wake forms behind the lure, the trick is not to lose your cool, just keep the retrieve coming and be ready. Once he has struck, keep him on the surface and coming to you to prevent his diving into the heavy stuff.

Large bass will be excited by an enticing bait and explode the surface to get a piece of it. At times, a pork eel or rubber grub can be added to surface offerings to increase their attractiveness. The trailer should increase the lure's action as it comes across the surface. Occasionally, allow the lure to descend into the openings of the dense cover. If a swirl is noticed while the bait is falling, a bass probably has it, so set the hook!

Snaking a spoon/eel combination over the surface above the hydrilla jungles can bring up fish you may never see otherwise. The average size of bass that eat these lures is usually large. Small bass don't seem to have the courage to attack them.

A spinnerbait can be effective in submerged cover that is only of medium density. It must have only a single blade attached via a good ball-bearing swivel. A short arm, drop-type spinnerbait with a weedless single hook is most effective. The lure should be balanced to drop straight on a free fall into a pocket among the heavy cover. Adding a larger blade to the spinnerbait will slow its descent without loss of control.

The Lunker Lure and Norman's Triple-Wing Buzz Bait are very popular baits with a blade design which pops them to the surface, allowing the fisherman to crank them back on top at a very slow pace. They can be used around dense moss and should be fished with the rod tip held high. Again, begin reeling just before the lure hits the water so that it is always on the surface. The best retrieve is usually slow, but the lure speed can be increased to trigger bass into striking.

OTHER BETS

While many crankbaits are almost impossible to fish in hydrilla, the Rattle Trap is a good bet for bass. I normally rip them along as fast as I can reel, which keeps the lure out of the weeds and in the productive zone. You can't outcrank a bass. Boat lanes are a good place to toss a chrome or bone-colored plug since the traffic prevents hydrilla from growing into the lane.

A very productive lure for waters with heavy submerged vegetation is the surface spinner bait. These areas are usually "home" to large populations of bass.

A 1/4 ounce slip sinker in front of a six inch purple worm is often productive. Any heavier weight and the bait will sink into the hydrilla. Watch the line, but leave a slight amount of slack so you can feel the fish without it feeling you. Bass hold tight here, and you can't be hasty in the retrieve.

Casts should be made as short as is practical and ahead of the boat as you work the fringes of the weeds so that the line of retrieve will not loop behind the boat. This allows better lure control and a better hook set when needed. Guiding your lure through ideal spots in heavy submerged vegetation takes practice.

Thick bogs of weeds above and below the surface provide bass with forage and protection in subdued lighting. The successful angler should keep his casts short to have a better chance at landing the big largemouth.

In heavy cover with just a few pockets of open water, bass will seldom have time to carefully examine the lure and will strike instinctively, often missing the lure. Lunker bass are particularly hard to land from an aquatic jungle, but having a lure that will work well to provoke the strike is a major consideration. Once that is accomplished, then you can work on getting him out of the entanglements.

Without the right technique for hydrilla fishing, a 20 fish per day trip may be only a two fish day. Boat position is especially critical in fishing waters full of hydrilla. Boat movement should be minimal to prevent hangups. Positioning affects lure control, which in turn affects the live well.

For an angler who learns to adapt to it, fishing in and around this submerged cover can be fantastic. It sometimes requires more patience and perseverance than fishing easier spots, but the rewards are there.

CHAPTER 10

FLOATING COVER

THE GREEN CANOPY CONNECTION

HEAVY AQUATIC COVER is a prime ingredient in the game plan of many shallow water bassmen. Hyacinths, lettuce, duckweed, smartweed, and the smaller-leafed pennywort are favorite bass holding structures and, surprisingly to some, fish can be easily pulled out from under most floating vegetation.

Floating plants send off shoots from a main root system, and when separated, will form a second root system and a second plant. The floating qualities of such plants enable them to spread by wind and currents, where they can quickly jam any bottleneck on the water system. For example, it doesn't take long for the water hyacinth to spread, since a single plant is capable of producing 50 thousand new plants each year.

Top water plants normally will spread until they are trapped or contained. They can be contained in emergent vegetation or structure, such as lily pads (in 3-5 feet of water), bullrushes (in 3-8 feet of water), and partially submerged trees (in 5-25 feet of water). The root mass of floating plants holds plenty of food for game fish. Crayfish, bugs, grass shrimp, and other forage are abundant in and below the dense floating mats. Bass and other game fish often feed under the shaded canopy.

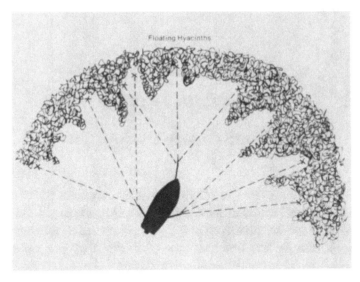

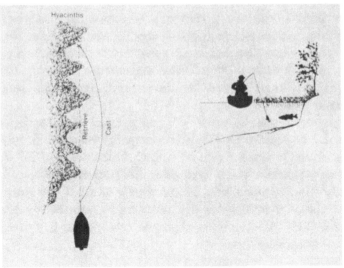

FIGURE 14 — *When casting to beds of floating vegetation, get the lure far back into the corners, cuts or slots. A crankbait retrieved parallel to the weedline can pay off with big dividends. Bring it back underneath any weed points that jut out, by manipulating your rod tip.*

Floating plants are nomads and can be found over any kind of bottom. If the plants get too populous and then die off and sink, the sediment can easily pile up on the lake's bottom. This sediment warms up the water in the winter, while the floating plant shade cools the shallow water in the summer.

Also, bass and other fish need rooted plants, such as maidencane, for spawning cover. Floaters can crowd out desirable vegetation and prosper on the water's excessive nutrients.Florida's Lake Tohopekaliga, for example, is on a downhill slide once again since its last drawdown (1979), and fishery biologists believe that the ominous aspect of a smartweed infestation throughout thousands of acres of shallow water is proving that. Fish population studies there, incidentally, support the theory.

WATER HYACINTH HIDEAWAYS

The "infamous" water hyacinth has spread over southern waters since its introduction in 1884 from South America. Eichornia crassipes has broad, shiny, dark green leaves and bluish-white flowers. They blow into shallow waters creating fish habitat in areas previously devoid of cover and in so doing, prove to be an excellent fish magnet.

If there is a predominant wind in the area, then start your search on the shallow, windward shoreline. The wind can pile plenty of the floating plants or pieces of plants into coves or lake arms. Baitfish, grass shrimp, and various forms of insects are also pushed into the area where hungry bass feed.

Hyacinths attract aquatic activity, which is a good sign. The best combination of aquatic life, according to many guides, is turtles, frogs, alligators, and hyacinths. Turtle activity is important, because they feed after a forage spree by the bass.

A creek or canal inlet or a river bed, may have adequate aquatic activity and some current regardless of the hyacinths. That's the secret to finding productive, shallow offshore structure that usually holds big fish in tighter schools.

111

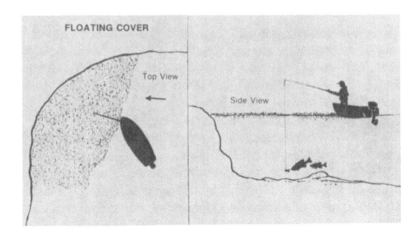

FIGURE 15 — *Water hyacinths can pile up on the windward shore and provide a home for hungry predators. Many anglers don't realize that the pockets just inside the weed edge are often free of underwater hang-ups. A weedless jig or worm rig dropped into these holes will entice a lot of bass.*

Heavy surface cover like parrot's feather can hide a lot of big bass. There could be concentrations of largemouth awaiting the angler who can get his bait back to them.

I look for active fish in hyacinths offshore. If the bass are moving quickly with the lure or bait, they are in a feeding mode and interested in keeping their "forage" away from a competitor. If the bass swim out from the heavy cover to deeper, open water, they are probably members of a school. When an area with such enthusiastic bass is located, it's often possible to catch well over your limit from the same hole.

BIRD TRAFFIC TIP

One thing to be aware of when searching out bass in floating vegetation of any kind is bird traffic. If there are birds feeding and walking around on the aquatic jungle, then there must also be small bugs, worms, etc. being jarred from those plants. The older a mat of plants is, the more food will be present. Birds are a key to finding some of the better weed clogs where large bass lurk.

Another bass benefit you may discover under these birds are lunkers eager for a feathered meal. Bass will definitely attack birds when possible, and I've seen some swirls and splashes beneath birds that were tip-toeing along over the water plants. Usually, they'll miss their targets, but if you're quick, you can place an accurate cast close to the action and maybe score.

The insect-hunting birds will tip you off to the bait fish and the bass. Egrets and herons near a plant jungle usually indicates minnows are present beneath the plants.

The key to finding big bass underneath hyacinths is to find areas where structure lies beneath it. The more permanent the hyacinth jam, the better the shallow water fishing will be. Any non-visible structure beneath the floating plants can only help the stringer. Hyacinths that move from one side of the lake to another as wind dictates may be devoid of good fish.

WEATHER FACTORS

Most dead hyacinths found on a lake or stream got that way from either very low (cold) temperatures or chemical spraying, and knowing the reason is very important in finding the best bass fishing areas. Herbicide spraying tends to be very spotty. The plants turn brown and then fall to the bottom to form a sludge. After a spraying, the bass will vacate the area and stay gone for several weeks.

Winter kill, on the other hand, is generally all inclusive. All plants from the shore or bank will turn brown at the same time, leaving only a perimeter of live plants farthest from shore. Winter kill doesn't necessarily shut off the fishing.

LURE RESEMBLANCE

Crankbaits that resemble crayfish, a favorite forage of bass, are a good choice around hyacinths. The plants are loaded with grass shrimp and small crayfish. Cast behind a hyacinth jam and bring the lure out underneath a corner. Bass will often stop it just as it leaves the shade. The wind or current will help in making the right cast and in controlling the retrieve.

Canal entrances, small tributaries, and runnoff areas that may have the floating plant trapped are great spots. These are natural places for feeding fish, and the hyacinths make it even more productive.

The relationship between the hyacinth and the structure below is the prime concern to many successful bass anglers. Points that are formed by the plant, as well as cuts through them, can be productive. Some anglers take their paddles and "notch" the weeds. After making a series of "pockets" in the cover, they back off and either cast lures or allow tail-hooked shiners to swim into the notches. The man-made pockets are especially suitable for live bait which can be controlled as it moves farther back under the mass of floating cover.

Canals, small tributaries, and other mini-waters with "clogs" of hyacinths are great spots to find schools of largemouth. Such places have a larger forage base than other, weed-free waters.

Texas-rigged worms fished at the edge of the hyacinth cover should be cast to hit on top of a plant. The weighted worm should ideally bounce and then fall between that plant and another. Bass will normally pick up the worm as it descends.

Since most floating plants are clumped together rather than floating individually, a weedline is formed, and an injured minnow plug is very productive in such areas. A slow, twitching retrieve is important to entice the bass out from under the floating mat.

Lures that create a fuss near a bed of floating plants or those which can be easily retrieved through them are most productive. While hang-ups may occur with the floating-minnow plug, it is often successful around such cover.

Small jigs designed primarily for crappie angling take many hauls of bass from floating cover. In clear water, the thick vegetation is used to mask the angler's approach, while stained water itself aids in camouflaging the boat. Holes are scooped in the cover and the small lures are jigged off the bottom in six or seven feet of water.

FLOATING SURFACE BLANKETS

Every cast gets fouled in the stuff. Even when a big bass explodes through it with his mouth wrapped around a plug, the aquatic plant is right in the middle of the action. Never mind though, largemouth don't seem to be overly concerned about floating "duck weed".

FIGURE 16 — *A lure retrieved through a blanket of duck weed should resemble forage trying to swim or crawl out on top of the weed. The strike will usually come as the lure drops back down or droops below this surface canopy.*

In fact, they love it. What may be considered a mild hassle to the plug tosser is certainly appealing to the largemouth clan. The constant plant "pest" that adorns each lure or bait that returns to the boat is a minute, one-eighth inch diameter plant that sits on the water's surface and drifts around with the wind. The microscopic, hair-like root structure on the "wet side" of each plant is not long

117

enough to intertwine, so duck weed must be considered as thousands of independently floating plants.

A predominant wind will normally result in a "floating skin" that is fairly tough to penetrate with a lure. The canopy actually "secures" the watery environment. The largemouth can freely roam beneath the cover and seek out forage, seemingly without apprehension.

Several factors enter into establishing a successful pattern with the "green blanket" loving largemouth. Weather, lake-bottom characteristics, and forage availability all affect appropriate tackle selection and the most productive presentations.

Duck weed exists on numerous waters around the country, and most bass anglers will come across it eventually if they visit many lakes. While it may not be commonly found in some parts, it is a fantastic "find" for those able to unlock its treasures.

SEMI-WEEDLESS FOOLERS

The successful angler will quickly establish the most productive ways to confront the bass beneath the duck weed canopies. The most successful lures, of course, are weedless, or in the case of duck weed, semi-weedless. The angler has to continuously overlook the few plants that always stick to the lure during a retrieve.

Bass are accustomed to seeing air-breathing forage scooting through or trying to walk over the stuff. While it's possible to get a lot of strikes and some hook-ups on almost any lure, some baits are more appropriate for the action. Catching fish on the surface is always exciting, but when they blow a big "hole" in the green blanket, look out. It's a nerve-jangling experience.

A weedless spoon dropped through the stuff and retrieved back just below the canopy works well. The lure's nose dimples the surface blanket as the spoon is retrieved through the dense shoreline cover.

Fishing duckweed is a unique experience for most anglers. For those that cast far back into it without worry about the lure collecting debris, the shallow water rewards are usually great.

I caught several largemouth on a dangling rear-end plug, called Top Dog. The Burke lure and a weedless spoon have a common trait that is vital to success on the near-surface feeding bass under the duck weed, and that is, action on the surface, yet visibility below. The largemouth can see what is making all the commotion. An attraction that few bass can resist is a mostly weed-free lure hanging below the canopy.

The Texas-rigged worm is productive only with a pegged slip sinker that is heavy enough to first punch a hole through the surface cover and then to maintain enough tension on the line for it to "cut" through the weed blanket on the retrieve. The worm can then be crawled along the underwater structure without significant interference from the surface canopy.

Most anglers exposed to duck weed and other floating plants, will leave them alone and go the other way. Casts to the weed line may result in a few bass, but the majority of fish, the large concentrations, are back under the stuff. Anglers often are lazy and won't try to figure out the best way to reach the fish under those circumstances. That's why there are so many largemouth in such places.

CHAPTER 11

EMERGENT PLANT LIFE

BETWIXT BONNETS AND BUGGY WHIPS

WE'VE ALL SEEN the shallow expanses of aquatic plant life that appears impenetrable to an angler's lure. Many fishermen will simply fish near the "jungle" and not in it. They are afraid of getting hung up, losing or fouling lures, and possibly losing any bass that may strike the offering.

Numerous strikes that occur in dense, emergent weed masses are misses, but such shallow water areas harbor exceptional concentrations of largemouth. Algae scum, dollar weed, spatterdock, and even fragrant water lilies can grow into masses of vegetation so thick that only a few small pockets exist.

The light below is subdued, but a lure's movement above does not go unnoticed. If the bait is kept moving across the weeds, it will attract attention. When it falls into a "hole" in the mass and touches water, hang on to the rod. Experience can teach you to perfect a retrieve over such cover and take advantage of the bass below.

To effectively catch your share, position the boat close to the shallow weed mass that you intend to fish. Your cast should be fairly short, so that you can maintain a good degree of accuracy and proper control of the lures as they're retrieved. The dense cover allows you to move in tighter on the quarry, and the odds of landing the bass improve as the length of line out decreases.

The better reed growth is on firm, sand bottoms and that's where the big bass can be found. The dense cover allows the angler to move in tighter to the "home" of many lunkers.

The tiny openings or small pockets are where the majority of strikes will occur. Cast a weedless lure beyond the target opening to avoid spooking any nearby inhabitant. Inch the lure to the edge of the pocket and let it free fall to the bottom. Most strikes will occur on the fall. Watch the lure as it is crawled along on top of the mass and the line when the bait falls into a "hole".

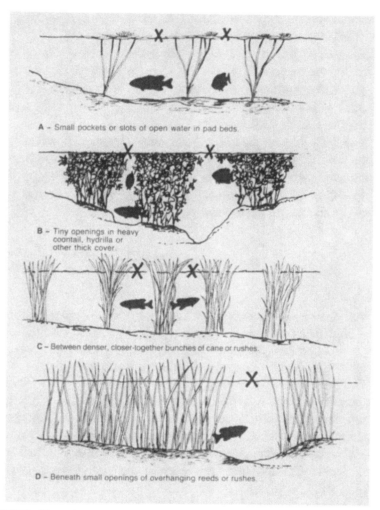

FIGURE 17 — *In most shallow, fertile waters, profuse emergent vegetation serves as home for numerous largemouth bass during the warmer months. Often, this vegetation encompasses more volume at the surface and leaves less dense cover nearer the bottom. A very effective way to get at these "buried" bass is to work a lure slowly through the pockets and small holes of open surface water within the vegetation.*

123

Use a good quality, low stretch monofilament line in 14 to 20 pound test here, if after trophy bass. The tackle needs to be heavy to withstand the fishing and catching conditions. A stiff rod to set the hook and jerk the lure free of trash is vital. The reel preferred by most weed-bound anglers is a heavy bait casting model.

One lure which is most often productive in this habitat is the plastic worm rigged "Texas style", or self-weedless. It can be worked with or without a slip sinker, but any weight should be "pegged" with a toothpick for optimum results. Use as light a sinker as possible in such shallow cover.

Weedless jig and eels are sometimes effective in this shallow habitat, and of course the weedless spoon has a well-deserved reputation for attracting weed-bound largemouth. Don't worry about getting debris on the lure, worry about hanging on to the rod when the bait drops into an open water pocket.

DENSE STAND FLIPPIN'

Tall emergent vegetation, such as bullrushes, cattails, and reeds, offers bass heavy cover in which to bury themselves. The dense stands of aquatic weeds that often grow to eight feet above the surface are the home of many concentrations of largemouth.

The primary way to effectively fish such areas is by flippin', or swinging a weedless lure into an opening in the stands. While many anglers back off from these stands, fearing constant hangups, the "flippers" move their boats in tight to the cover and, while standing, wave their long, seven-foot rods in an effort to dunk their bait into a bass hideout. With practice, they learn to flip the lure in all potential pockets with few snags.

A weedless jig or Texas-rigged worm is employed in the technique, which consists of vertically jigging the lure up and down, eight to ten times in each hole in the stand. When the bass are concentrated in shallow water under thickly matted reeds, it is possible to catch three or four largemouth from a single "hole". The angler finding a weed-bound school won't have to move his boat far to take advantage of the circumstances.

124

Huge largemouth bury themselves in dense emergent vegetation. Flippin' a weighted worm into a clump of bullrushes can often provide a fisherman with the battle of his life.

125

The plastic worm with a large tail is a popular lure to drop into the thick of things. One very important trick to use on the flippin' worm rig concerns the slip sinker. In such dense cover, it cannot be left to free-slide. It must be pegged by inserting a round toothpick into the sinker and breaking off the tip to wedge the line and "weld" the worm and weight together. This will prevent their parting company when the rig is worked in the dense cover.

The worm can be oiled heavily with a fish attractor solution to facilitate ease of sliding in and out of the weed stands. A dry, flexible plastic worm may grab each and every stalk of reed as the bait is removed from a "dry" hole. Lubrication is an important aspect to consider in flippin', to keep down the "frustration factor'"

The method is hard work, but for those bass concentrations in dense, shallow stands of cover, this is often the most effective way to catch them. The trolling motor can be run seemingly within inches of the weed-lover without spooking the fish. Reeds and other tall vegetation can be more closely watched for bass movement when the boat is near them.

When the reeds or bullrushes are thick with bass, the successful angler will move in next to the stand and flip his weedless bait into the tiny pockets. The trolling motor can be run right up to the cover without spooking the fish.

126

Aquatic vegetation research by fisheries biologists, relative to bass presence, has been revealing. Shocking studies have found that bullrushes are generally preferred over cattails. The reasons may be two-fold. Bullrush communities tend to be less dense than cattails, and bass can move in and out of them more easily. Bullrushes also produce more invertebrates.

The flippin' technique is around to stay. It is the top method under specific "jungle" conditions, and those will not change in our lifetime.

POKING PADS

Bass often prefer a pad-type cover over other types of emergent vegetation. There are several kinds of aquatic pads.

Spatterdock, which has an oval shaped leaf and yellow blossoms, is very common in many states. It requires high pH (acidic water) and the leaves have the notorious splits that can create hang-ups. The leaves are above water, but they overlap and harbor more bugs than other types. Bugs light on the leaves (or stems) and attract forage fish which, in turn, bring bass.

The fragrant water lily has a round leaf and a white flower. Like the spatterdock, the fragrant water lily has overlapping leaves and lots of small bugs. Sunfish will come up under a leaf and suck a bug right through it! So checking out such pad areas for leaves having small pin holes will aid in determining the population of bream and reveal the potential for bass.

Another type of pad is the lotus, which the winter cold normally kills off each year. It comes back in the spring though, and its leaves do not have splits, making it an easier pad to fish. In the spring, new lotus shoots attract fish. Dollar bonnets are found primarily in extremely shallow water and are not a significant factor in most bass fishing.

There are several considerations in the lure selection for heavy pad cover. The preferred lures will have only a single weedless hook. For heavy lily pad beds, something with a round nose up front should be selected so that it can scoot through the pad slits. Your line

127

will eventually fall into the slits and a square front end on the lure won't allow it to forge on through, without a lot of force.

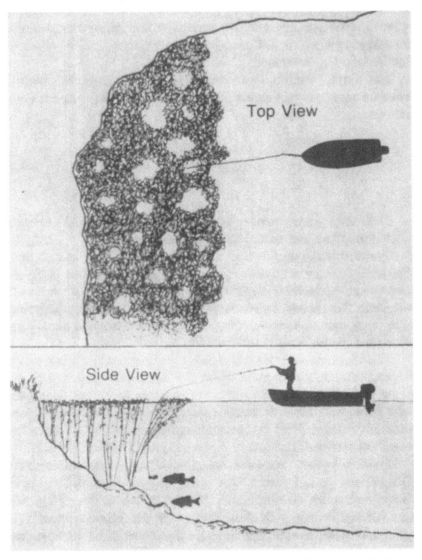

FIGURE 18 — *Heavy, surface-blanketing cover such as lily pads can be heaven for bass. The open water below is shaded, cool, and gives the bass lots of room to roam in search of forage.*

The most preferable lures for heavy cover should be fairly light so that they will bounce along on top of the cover and get hung up less often. The lure should also have some bulk so that it knocks on the cover, telegraphing mealtime to the lunkers below. This commotion will drive bass crazy, so look out when your lure drops into an opening. In waters with such cover, both you and the bass have to rely on sound much more than sight.

SHORELINE SNEAKING

Emergent weedbeds begin at the shore and extend out into the water for several feet. This doesn't always eliminate the non-boaters catching a few shallow, weed-loving largemouth.

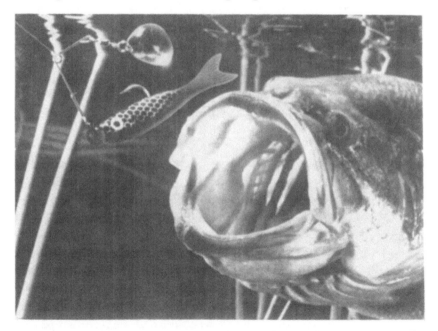

Various forms of aquatic vegetation harbor weed-bound bass year round. The thicker the below-water mass of weeds, the more productive, usually, if you can effectively fish it. That plant portion seen above the waterline is not necessarily indicative of what is below.

Heavy cover often replaces depth in the requirements of bass. Tall, shoreline weed beds provide bass with security of sorts, and forage aplenty. To the bass, it is an enticing, food-intensive environment that provides ambush cover in the shallows.

Hang-ups may result in lost lures more often than for the boat angler, but the person on shore will get his share of bass with a little persistence. Weeds nearer the shore are generally thicker and bass generally concentrate in the thickest patch available. A bank angler using some stealth can approach to within casting distance of these fish. Using shoreline cover to hide his presence, the successful bank angler moves quietly, casting to nearby "pockets" that a boat angler may overlook.

Areas where the weeds are different in some way are particularly active bass haunts. An expanse of maidencane, with an isolated patch or two of pickerel weed, would be an example. The bass concentrations would most probably be in the dense pickerel patch. The successful bank caster will check out the depressions, slots, points, boat lanes, clearing, etc., in and around the shallow weed cover.

TROLLING TACTICS

Various forms of vegetation grow until the mass is so dense that it is virtually impenetrable for predator and angler. In such clogs, bass often stick close to the outside edge, or weedline. Largemouth are able to ambush their prey by holding tight to the thick weed mass.

In such locations, they are also prone to strike at a trolled lure. An angler can cover territory quickly with the aid of an outboard or powerful electric motor. The lure or bait can be presented to numerous bass along a weedline. The key to successful trolling is in the speed of the boat adjacent to a weedline and the resultant position of a lure at all times in bass striking territory.

Irregular spots along a weedline are great places to hook up with a largemouth. Both pockets and points entice this predator to lie in wait for its food. Bass, particularly big ones, will "stake out" such preferred territories along a shallow weedline.

Weeds will often grow to a drop off and stop. Other limiting factors to their multiplication in a lake or river is water clarity, fertility, and type of soil. Regardless, finding bass along a weedline via trolling is viable during all but the coldest months.

Either lures or baits can be trolled. One successful guide I know uses king-size shiners and his electric motor to attract huge largemouth. Other productive trollers use Rattletraps which can be "ripped" free of most weed hangups. Shallow diving plugs can be speed-trolled along the weedline. Not only are these lures effective at finding bass, but they will also tell you exactly what vegetation is below.

CHAPTER 12

BRUSHY STRUCTURES

BLOW-OVERS AND INUNDATED TIMBER

SUBMERGED TREES exist in most shallow waterways. Inclement weather such as tornadoes, water spouts, and hurricanes, and plain old age can frequently knock down trees in a body of water. And, these areas are magnets to bass.

Trees often collapse leaving few fragments to find above water, and thus, surface keys may be non-existent. Generally, however, a few trees are left standing in shallow water, and this is a prime place to start searching for bass.

Floods, in particular, have a similar effect on rivers; banks are undercut by high waters and trees topple. Also, some lakes that were logged by lumbermen during a period of drought and low water, may have many shallow water stumps. In many areas, lake bottoms are covered with stumps, and no apparent traces are noted on the surface. A depth finder with shallow water transducer can pick these up.

Flooded trees and brush may be full of shallow water bass and other game fish, yet many anglers are unsuccessful at fishing them. Other fishermen generally avoid such areas due to the potential problems associated with fishing in the heavy structure. Hang-ups and lost tackle are a reality, and a day in the (submerged) woods can be a frustrating and expensive experience for some people.

Proper boat and lure control are indeed difficult in submerged timber, but one has to become proficient at both to catch fish that hold on the structure below. Using the emergent timber to help determine the structure beneath should aid the angler who can't catch bass without actually seeing a target.

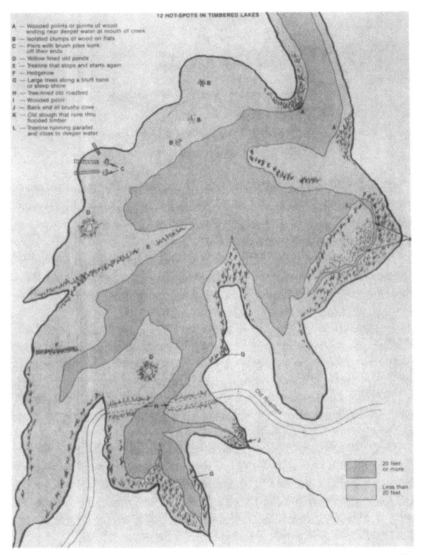

FIGURE 19 — *Shallow timber exists in most waters and "collects" bass. The options are numerous if you know where to look.*

Bass need something to relate to, even in the brush and submerged trees. Any elevation change that runs through such terrain may provide the proper structure. The stable conditions of

134

summertime allow the bass to move onto the gradual sloping breaks within the trees. In the winter though, bass frequent extremely sharp breaks near the edge of shallow, flooded timber. They have to make severe adjustments at times due to the weather, and can move to deeper, warmer water easily.

Once a concentration of shallow water bass is located, speed control is the key to large stringers. Clear-water fish may feed by sight, but in murky, brush-filled water, sound, vibration, and speed are more important.

LOGICAL LOCATIONS

Shallow brush provides cover, protection, and food, and it may even have an influence on water temperature and current flow. Submerged timber and limbs can be found in most lakes and rivers, whether they are man-made reservoirs or natural bodies.

Timber areas have been left standing in most reservoirs constructed in the past several years for fish management purposes. These areas can be spotted emerging from the water's surface in shallow coves off the lake's main body. Natural waters have vast areas of submerged brush.

The lake run-in (or run-off) from tributaries generally contains good fish, and many shallow water bass will position themselves at a point formed by trees, near a drop in depth. The mouths of creeks or rivers should generally be fished from the lake side. An angler should work the brushy points in six or seven feet of water first and then gradually move shallower and on into the tributary, in search of the strike.

Isolated clumps of submerged trees or brush sometimes concentrate and hold the structure-oriented largemouth bass. Those locations are very productive, and this type of structure on a break or change in bottom elevation can be easily found with a depth flasher. Most anglers will work the shallow brush edges first and then move to the heavy stuff in the middle.

Timber areas left standing in many waters are usually the home of bass. Shallow coves may have a variety of brush forms including stick-ups, blow-downs, etc., and figuring out the productive pattern is the key to fun.

A stand of old, flooded willow trees, shaped in a circle, generally tips off an angler to the presence of a submerged farm pond. Where willows are found, water could have never been far away. The presence of a group of emergent willows (or others) in the shape of a semicircle or quarter moon may also indicate the submerged dam area of what was once a pond or small lake.

Trees or brush may start in shallow water and then continue into the depths. This provides a definite migration route for bass to move to shallower water when feeding. The tree line may break up at the surface in places, but scanning the lake should tip off an observant angler to what's beneath. Not all tree tops have to be emergent in shallow water to provide a good migration path. It's what is below that counts. Start fishing the shallower structure first in the spring and fall months.

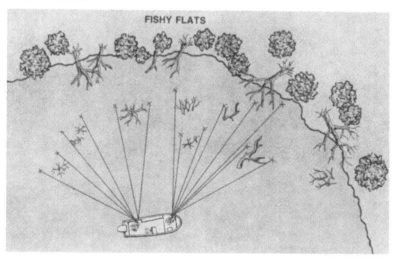

FIGURE 20 — *The most productive flats are those laden with submerged brush. Cast to the thickest bunches of timber. Dingy water areas in the backs of shallow, brushy coves will often hold bass all day under many conditions.*

The backs of shallow, brushy coves with a fresh source of water are often productive and should be checked out. Any break provided by a creek channel in shallow trees should be worked first, since bass may be near the drop (into the creek bed) unless they have moved shallow in an explosive feeding mode.

Wooded points are often good areas to search for all bass species: smallmouth, largemouth, and spotted. A shallow, wooded point is generally better than one without brush. Bass will move from deeper water, up the point and, at a given time, can usually be found somewhere along it, be it 3 feet or 7 feet.

137

Brushy structure is a great place to find large concentrations of bass. Cast a bait to timber-strewn waters and hang on to the rod.

Lining Up The Largemouth

Bass move along underwater "routes" in search of shallow water food. Many of those paths have associated timber or brush present. For example, old roadbeds may exist in many man-made impoundments around the country. Ditches often separate the road bed from tree rows along the submerged path, and bass utilize such areas in their movements. Many times, the old road can be seen entering the lake on each side of a cove.

Flooded "hedge rows" exist in many reservoirs and bass generally love these thickets. The trees that hold the most forage for shallow water bass are very dense. They existed on farm land prior to the lake's impoundment and were planted to prevent wind erosion and damage to crop lands.

An angler can start fishing on one end of a tree row and work it to the shallows. Casts should be parallel to the edge and back into the row, while maneuvering the boat along within ten feet or so of the trees.

An old slough or canal may exist, and both natural waters and reservoirs contain these secret "hideaways". An angler may have to look through a lot of flooded timber before finding this type of water, but once he does, the topographical change is usually well defined. These areas often provide quiet angling protected from the wind and other fishermen.

A tree line ends for a reason (usually a change in elevation) and it can be easily fished. A boat with anglers working their lures parallel to the edge of the flooded forest will usually produce more than one whose anglers are casting perpendicular to it. In the fall or spring, when sudden weather changes may occur, bass prefer to frequent such places. They'll want to descend fast when a cold snap hits and won't have to travel far if the nearby drop is sharp.

Spoon Feeding

Heavy timber in a reservoir or natural body of water not only provides the fish with plenty of cover and food but helps to camouflage the approach of an angler. Evidence of the fisherman is filtered through the trees to the fish. It is normally possible to work very close to heavy, shallow structure without "spooking" the largemouth.

A particularly effective way to fish the flooded jungles is with the "timber spoon" method. It is very productive during fall, spring, and even in mid-summer, when the bass are back in the underwater woods.

The tackle used in this technique consists of a good, stiff action rod, baitcasting reel, tough 20-pound test monofilament line, and a dozen spoons (you may need more). The heavy line may save some lures and will allow an angler to bring his catch in quickly, giving it little time to escape. A split ring is commonly used to tie to in order to increase the spoon's action, and sharp hooks are a must. The large trebles on some spoons can be easily replaced with single hooks which will lessen the probability (and eventuality) of hangups.

The spoon is allowed to fall to the bottom into likely looking structure, five to eight feet deep. A slow, pumping motion is used to lift and drop the spoon. The lure should fall on a taut line so that a strike can be felt. Most strikes will come at this time. Too slow a fall won't fool the bass, and of course, too slack a line won't relay the strike quickly enough.

Even shallow, flooded "jungles" look different when the water drops to expose the full "reality". Try to check out such places during low water periods and then return when the water returns.

141

BASS ACCOMMODATIONS

On southern lakes, partially standing cypress trees may be the rule rather than the exception. Natural causes can pile up broken limbs and the upper portions of tree trunks on the bottom. Areas such as this usually hold resident bass, and an angler only has to look for evidence of broken limbs.

Fishing cypress knees with a Texas-rigged worm can sometimes be difficult, but patience is the key to finding bass in these areas. The trees grow in shallow depths, but the ones in the deepest water generally house the most bass. Isolated trees, in particular, hold bass that are usually larger than those in extremely shallow water.

The hardest part of any shallow water brush method is determining the strike. The tree limbs can create havoc, but the old adage "practice makes perfect" is valid here. Once the lure or bait has successfully enticed a nice stringer of bass from the shallows, most anglers will soon again head to the woods!

CHAPTER 13

MAN-MADE "OBSTRUCTIONS"

FROM THE UNIQUE TO THE COMMON

FISH WILL USUALLY be found shallower than you would normally expect in a lake, if they're using man-made "obstructions". Food, cover, and protection are what bass demand, and these shallow water structure types provide it.

Man-made objects are often overlooked, and they can be great. Many lakes have little natural structure, and a created "obstruction" is an almost certain place to catch some nice bass. Depending on the availability of deep water elsewhere, they can hold bass for a couple of hours or for months.

Bass do not generally inhabit barren, muck-laden bottoms in deep water. They will usually "relate" to something, and piers, pilings and docks may prove to be key areas. Don't assume that piers and pilings located in 3 to 4 feet of water are too shallow to hold any fish. If they come close enough to relatively deeper waters, they will.

Long piers may house many fish. Bass will move along them and into nearby weedbeds, on feeding movements. For this reason, weedbeds or other natural structure adjacent to docks and piers, can be especially productive during feeding activity.

Piers and docks naturally attract baitfish and bass can't be far away. Long, man-made structures may be obvious, but many bass fishermen overlook the full expanse.

PIER MOVEMENT

When bass schools begin a feeding migration, a few fish will hold on certain structure along the route before moving shallower. Normally, big bass concentrations will move toward the shallows en masse to feed along established paths. What better defined path could there be than a long pier?

Shallow water bass can often be found using such structure, if the angler knows where to look. Certain structures, floating and supported, are much better than others, and attention to the differences will result in heavier stringers.

Dock owners often try to create a holding area for fish beneath their docks by dropping brush beside the pilings. Naturally, baitfish congregate in these areas and "draw" crappie, bluegill, and largemouth bass.

A key factor in determining the better docks to fish is the algae growth present on the walkway crossmembers and supports. The more algae present and the longer the pilings have been in the water, the better your chances of finding an "old" bass home.

I try to move along a pier slowly. If I move by quickly and only make a few casts, then I'll often be missing fish. Don't believe that all the bass will be out on the end of the pier in the deepest water! Many times I've caught them in the middle of the pier's length, in extremely shallow water.

Man-made wood such as bulkheads and pilings provide habitat for micro-organisms which start the food chain that leads to bass. Fish the entire length of any row of pilings to reep the full benefits.

TACKLE TIPS

Fishing heavy pilings requires heavy line and good equipment. Most fish will try to do "figure 8's" around the submerged posts when they catch up with the bait. Because of this, it is necessary to hit the bass fast and "horse" it out. Tackle not up to the task is useless in most cases.

I normally prefer 14 or 17 pound test monofilament line when fishing wood objects. My level wind reels and heavy action rods handle the line and bass for which I'm fishing. Very seldom will a bass grab the lure and run directly toward you (and away from the structure), but it does happen. Usually, you will need heavy equipment to prevent entanglements and a breakoff.

I remember tossing a tandem-hooked worm rig to a river piling once. A bass, suspended in the cool shade of the wooden pier, sucked the black worm into her mouth. On the other end of the line, I felt the pickup and set back on the rod.

She powered the rod almost to a horizontal position before the drag screamed. The battle continued as I regained a few feet of line, but the bass then darted around the post and became snagged. I then reeled the rod into the water and tried to poke it free, assuming that the second hook on the rigged worm had become embedded in the wooden post. That didn't work.

Minutes passed as I thought about my options. I continued to feel the surge of the largemouth and wanted to get a good look at her. Finally, I exerted pressure on the line, the snagged hook gave way and I hoisted the six pounder into the boat.

The fish, not large by most standards, was a decent anchor for my day's string of nine bass. All were pulled from a man-made, wood environment.

Man has constructed fish homes on most waters in this country and such structure in a shallow lake or pond can be very productive. Wormin' the piers is a favorite pastime of the author.

PLASTIC AND RUBBER

Normally, I use a Fishin' Worm Salty Sensation when pier or dock fishing because of its enticing action at very slow speeds. The majority of times, the bass will pick up the plastic bait as it plummets to the bottom on the initial cast to that area.

Occasionally, the bass will hit just as the bottom hugger leaves the pier and heads for open water. A chief advantage is that the worm can be fished slowly and kept in the prime zone for several seconds. The plastic bait is, in my opinion, the most productive pier, dock, or piling fishing lure.

Crank baits too are very effective around pilings and piers at certain times. I work my favorite shad models at a "hard crank" speed and have been especially successsful with them early and late in the day.

In many lakes throughout the country, shallow water piers, docks, and pilings exist in great quantities, and usually bass are abundant around them. In waters with little other shallow structure, these wood "attractors" are the place to go for bass.

In shallow waters, boat houses attract largemouth and more importantly, their forage. Vegetation added to the wood cover makes such places great bass holes.

BEING DIFFERENT

Several other unique obstructions provide a home for bass. None should be overlooked when trying to establish a productive pattern. Often, the uncommon types of shallow habitat yield healthy strings of bass when others won't.

- Shiner traps are utilized extensively in some shallow waters to capture shiners for use as bass bait. Baitfish are drawn by a chum into the net traps which are placed on long poles stuck into the river or lake bed. The chum, composed of bread dough, wheat, or some other grain product, is scattered into the area to attract the forage. Bass should be near.

- Concrete, wood, rock, and metal bulkheads prohibit wave, current, or wind action from washing away shoreline and forcing relatively deeper banks to become shallow. They also prohibit encroachment of smaller aquatic life into extreme shallow water to escape their predators. This containment concentrates the bait and aids bass interested in the small food morsels, to easily capture the unwary.

- Water flow control gates, dams, locks, and spillways all function in a manner to control the water level on one side. They also release (at some time) water on the downstream side and the effect on bass and an angler's live well can be fantastic. Bait fish will congregate in shallow areas below these structures when there is some flowage of water. A periodic opening and closing of water control gates can ring a dinner bell for the largemouth.

- Barges, boats, and other floating craft are very prone to sinking during heavy rains or storms, and once they do, many are abandoned. Excellent structure is often available, and many such "wrecks" can be observed partially projecting above the surface.

- Duck blinds, permanently located in shallow waters throughout the country, aren't just for ducks. Most of these structures are magnets for the largemouth bass. Metal blinds, stake blinds, and wire covered hideaways all produce excellent angling under the right conditions. Blinds built to handle (and hide) small duck boats usually have one side open and are so constructed that an angler can easily fish them.

- Bridges offer an increased flow rate in the area, relatively deeper water, reduced area of water (such as lake "necking" down) and good structure with marine growth. Evidence of the food cycle can be easily found in such an area. Bass will know that!

The successful angler may have to cast to the unique obstructions six or seven times before enticing a bass. When the bass does pick up the lure, it's then time to get his head up and head him out...toward the boat. There's no good time for an angler to "fool around" with a bass in man-made hazards.

BASS SERIES LIBRARY!

Eight Great Books With A Wealth Of Information For Bass Fishermen

By Larry Larsen

I. FOLLOW THE FORAGE FOR BETTER BASS ANGLING - VOLUME 1 BASS/PREY RELATIONSHIP - The most important key to catching bass is finding them in a feeding mood. Knowing the predominant forage, its activity and availability, as well as its location in a body of water will enable an angler to catch more and larger bass. Whether you fish artificial lures or live bait, you will benefit from this book.

SPECIAL FEATURES

o PREDATOR/FORAGE INTERACTION
o BASS FEEDING BEHAVIOR
o UNDERSTANDING BASS FORAGE
o BASS/PREY PREFERENCES
o FORAGE ACTIVITY CHART

II. FOLLOW THE FORAGE FOR BETTER BASS ANGLING - VOLUME 2 TECHNIQUES - Beginners and veterans alike will achieve more success utilizing proven concepts that are based on predator/forage interactions. Understanding the reasons behind lure or bait success will result in highly productive, bass-catching patterns.

SPECIAL FEATURES

o LURE SELECTION CRITERIA
o EFFECTIVE PATTERN DEVELOPMENT
o NEW BASS CATCHING TACTICS
o FORAGING HABITAT
o BAIT AND LURE METHODS

III. BASS PRO STRATEGIES - Professional fishermen have opportunities to devote extended amounts of time to analyzing a body of water and planning a productive day on it. They know how changes in pH, water temperature, color and fluctuations affect bass fishing, and they know how to adapt to weather and topographical variations. This book reveals the methods that the country's most successful tournament anglers have employed to catch bass almost every time out. The reader's productivity should improve after spending a few hours with this compilation of techniques!

SPECIAL FEATURES

o MAPPING & WATER ELIMINATION
o LOCATE DEEP & SHALLOW BASS
o BOAT POSITION FACTORS
o WATER CHEMISTRY INFLUENCES
o WEATHER EFFECTS
o TOPOGRAPHICAL TECHNIQUES

IV. BASS LURES - TRICKS & TECHNIQUES - Modifications of lures and development of new baits and techniques continue to keep the fare fresh, and that's important. Bass seem to become "accustomed" to the same artificials and presentations seen over and over again. As a result, they become harder to catch. It's the new approach that again sparks the interest of some largemouth. To that end, this book explores some of the latest ideas for modifying, rigging and using them. The lure modifications, tricks and techniques presented within these covers will work anywhere in the country.

SPECIAL FEATURES

o UNIQUE LURE MODIFICATIONS
o IN-DEPTH VARIABLE REASONING
o PRODUCTIVE PRESENTATIONS
o EFFECTIVE NEW RIGGINGS
o TECHNOLOGICAL ADVANCES

V. SHALLOW WATER BASS - Catching shallow water large-mouth is not particularly difficult. Catching lots of them usually is. Even more challenging is catching lunker-size bass in seasons other than during the spring spawn. Anglers applying the information within the covers of this book on marshes, estuaries, reservoirs, lakes, creeks or small ponds should triple their results. The book details productive new tactics to apply to thin-water angling. Numerous photographs and figures easily define the optimal locations and proven methods to catch bass.

SPECIAL FEATURES

o UNDERSTANDING BASS/COVER INTERFACE
o METHODS TO LOCATE BASS CONCENTRATIONS
o ANALYSIS OF WATER TYPES
o TACTICS FOR SPECIFIC HABITATS
o LARSEN'S "FLORA FACTOR"

VI. BASS FISHING FACTS - This angler's guide to the lifestyles and behavior of the black bass is a reference source of sorts, never before compiled. The book explores the behavior of bass during pre- and post-spawn as well as during bedding season. It examines how bass utilize their senses to feed and how they respond to environmental factors. The book details how fishermen can be more productive by applying such knowledge to their bass angling. The information within the covers of this book includes those bass species, known as "other" bass, such as redeye, Suwannee, spotted, etc.

SPECIAL FEATURES

o BASS FORAGING MOTIVATORS
o DETAILED SPRING MOVEMENTS
o A LOOK AT BASS SENSES
o GENETIC INTRODUCTION/STUDIES
o MINOR BASS SPECIES & HABITATS

VII. TROPHY BASS - is focused at today's dedicated lunker hunters who find more enjoyment in wrestling with one or two monster largemouth than with a "panfull" of yearlings. To help the reader better understand how to catch big bass, a majority of this book explores productive techniques for trophies. The "how to" information was gleaned from professional guides and other experienced trophy bass hunters. This book takes a look at the geographical areas and waters that offer better opportunities to catch giant bass.

SPECIAL FEATURES

o GEOGRAPHIC DISTRIBUTIONS
o STATE RECORD INFORMATION
o GENETIC GIANTS
o TECHNIQUES FOR TROPHIES
o LOCATION CONSIDERATIONS
o LURE AND BAIT TIMING

VIII. AN ANGLER'S GUIDE TO BASS PATTERNS examines the most effective combination of lure, method and places. Being able to develop a pattern of successful methods and lures for specific habitats and environmental conditions is the key to catching several bass on each fishing trip. Understanding bass movements and activities and the most appropriate and effective techniques to employ will add many pounds of enjoyment to the sport of bass fishing. "Bass Patterns" is a reference source for all anglers, regardless of where they live or their skill level.

SPECIAL FEATURES

o BOAT POSITIONING
o NEW WATER STRATEGIES
o DEPTH AND COVER CONCEPTS
o MOVING WATER TACTICS
o WEATHER/ACTIVITY FACTORS
o TRANSITIONAL TECHNIQUES

Breinigsville, PA USA
20 June 2010
240142BV00004B/3/P